B. M. EIKHENBAUM
LERMONTOV

A STUDY IN LITERARY-HISTORICAL EVALUATION
TRANSLATED BY RAY PARROTT AND HARRY WEBER

Ardis   Ann Arbor

Boris Eikhenbaum
LERMONTOV

English translation by Ray Parrott and Harry Weber

Copyright © 1981 by Ardis

Library of Congress Cataloging in Publication Data

Eikhenbaum, Boris Mikhailovich, 1886-1959.
    Lermontov: a study in literary-historical evaluation.

    Includes bibliographical references.
    1. Lermontov, Mikhail IUr'evich, 1814-1841–Criticism
and interpretation.
PG3337.L46E413   891.71'3   81-408
I SBN 0-88233-704-1   AACR1

The twin, and often incompatible, aims of fidelty to the original Russian and fluency in English guided our efforts in this translation. Nevertheless, we have sacrificed literalism whenever it hampered ease of reading and comprehension. With only a few exceptions our interpolations are encased in brackets. We took the liberty of breaking down many of Eikhenbaum's long sentences into shorter ones, and modifying his extensive use of colons and dashes to accord with accept English practices. In such instances we have provided coordinating and subordinating links to avoid ambiguity.

Footnotes 11 and 12 were missing in the original text; we have made every effort to restore them correctly to the appropriate passages.

* * * * *

A very special note of gratitude goes to Mary Lou Parrott for typing the manuscript and bearing up under all the attendant circumstances. We also wish to thank Nellie Weber and Miriam Gelfand for those numerous occasions when only an "informant's" grasp of the language could clear up the inevitable *tyomnye mesta;* their assistance has been invaluable. We, of course, assume full responsibility for any mistranslations which may still exist and any egregious choices in selecting from among variant readings.

Ray Parrott
Harry Weber

CONTENTS

To date Lermontov's creative work rarely has been interpreted as a literary historical fact. The traditional history of literature has regarded him only as a "reflection" of social moods, as a "confession of a member of the intelligentsia of the 30s and 40s"; other studies possess the character of impressionistic interpretations of a religio-philosophical or psychological type. Despite his extraordinary popularity, the revival of literary science begun some fifteen years ago in Russia has barely touched Lermontov. Apparently, this is explained by the fact that Lermontov does not stand in the rank of poets whose artistic influence has been clearly felt by the new generation and which once more has attracted the attention of critics and researchers. In the make-up of the literary traditions which formed Russian Symbolism, the name of Lermontov cannot stand alongside the names of Tyutchev and Fet, despite individual poet's attraction to him (especially Blok's).

Lermontov proved useful during the period of fascination with "Nietzscheanism" and "God-seeking" (Merezhkovsky, Zakrzhevsky), but that is all. This period passed and the question of Lermontov ceased to be immediate, although it remained unclear as before. The one-hundredth anniversary of Lermontov's birth, which coincided with the beginning of the European war (1914), did not introduce anything vitally new into the study of his creative work. The Academy edition of his work bypassed this literary historical problem, citing Belinsky's "brilliant appraisal" (as if the problem were a matter of a simple, aesthetic evaluation), and justified the omission by referring to the fact that posterity's conflicting opinions about the character and essence of Lermontov's poetry were "the best indicator of how much there is that is puzzling, unclear, and moot in the poet's multifaceted soul" (V, p. CXII).

Lermontov cannot be studied until the question about him is posed concretely and literarily-historically in the real sense of the word. Religio-philosophical and psychological interpretations of poetic creativity always will be and inevitably must be debatable and contradictory because they characterize not the poet but that historical moment which produced them. Time passes, and nothing remains of them except "debatable and conflicting judgements" prompted by the needs and tendencies of the epoch. One must not confuse a history of the understanding and interpretations of artistic works with the history of art proper. *To study* a poet's creative work does not mean simply to evaluate and interpret it, because in the first instance it is examined historically on the basis of special theoretical principles, and in the second, impressionistically, on the basis of premises of taste and world-outlook.

The real Lermontov is the *historical* Lermontov. To avoid misunderstandings, I must make the reservation that in saying this I do not at all mean Lermontov as an individual event in *time*--an event which simply has to be restored. Time and, by the same token, the concept of the past do not comprise the bases of historical knowledge. Time in history is a fiction, a convention which plays an auxiliary role. We are studying not motion in time, but motion as such: a *dynamic process* which in no way can be fragmented is never interrupted, and precisely for that reason does not possess actual time within itself and cannot be measured by time. Historical study reveals the dynamics of events, the laws of which operate not only within the limits of a conditionally selected epoch, but everywhere and always. In this sense, no matter how paradoxical it sounds, history is a science about the constant, the immutable, the motionless, although it concerns itself with change and motion. It can be a science only to the extent that it succeeds in converting real motion into a schema. Historical lyricism, like being in love with one or another epoch for its own sake, does not constitute a science. To study an event historically does not at all mean to describe it as an isolated instance which has meaning only in the conditions of its own time. This is a naive historicism which renders science sterile. It is not a matter of a simple *projection into the past*, but of understanding the historical *actuality* of an event, of determining its role in the development of historical energy, which, in its very essence, is constant, does not appear and disappear, and therefore operates outside of time. A historically understood fact by the same token is removed from time. Nothing repeats itself in history precisely because nothing vanishes, but only mutates. Therefore, historical analogies are not only possible but even necessary; and the study of historical events outside the historical process as individual, "unrepeatable" self-contained systems is impossible because it contradicts the very nature of these events.

"The historical Lermontov" is Lermontov *understood historically*--as a force entering into the general dynamics of its epoch, and, by the same token, generally into history as well. We study a historical individuality as it is expressed in creative work, and not a natural (psycho-physical) individuality, for which completely different materials must be adduced. The study of a poet's creative work as an immediate emanation of his soul or as a manifestation of his individual, self-contained "verbal consciousness" leads to the destruction of the very concept of individuality as a stable unit. Encountering the variety and changeability or contradictoriness of styles within the limits

10

of individual creativity, investigators are forced to qualify almost all writers as "dual" natures: Pushkin, Gogol, Lermontov, Tyutchev, Turgenev, Tolstoy Dostoevsky, etc., all have passed through this qualification. Together with "demonism" in Lermontov one finds "blueness" (see S. Durylin's article in *Russkaya mysl,* 1914, X), because in his work not only eyes, the sky and the steppes, but even the stars are "blue." On this path of "immanent" interpretations we have reached an impasse, and no compromises on a linguistic or any other basis can help. We must decisively reject these attempts which are dictated by world-view or polemical biases.

* * * * * *

The literary epoch to which Lermontov belonged (the 1830s and 40s) had to resolve the struggle between poetry and prose, a struggle which clearly had developed by the mid-20s. It was impossible to proceed further on the basis of those principles which had shaped Russian poetry at the beginning of the 19th century and which had created the verse of Pushkin. It was necessary to find new aesthetic norms and expressive means for verse because nothing other than feeble imitation could appear on the former course. There came a period of a lowering of poetic style, a decline of the high lyrical genres, the victory of prose over verse, the novel over the poem. Poetry had to be given more "content," to be made more programmatic, the verse as such less noticeable; it was necessary to intensify the emotional and ideational motivation of poetic speech in order to justify anew its very existence. As always in history, this process develops not in the form of a single line of facts, but in the complex form of an interweaving and contrasting of diverse traditions and methods; it is the struggle between these elements which shapes the epoch. The supremacy of one method or style arises as the result of this struggle--as a victory--after which a decline invariably follows. Other poets are acting simultaneously with Pushkin, not only those who are associated with him but also those who proceed by different paths unrelated to Pushkin: not only Vyazemsky, Baratynsky, Delvig, Yazykov, etc., but also Zhukovsky, and Tyutchev, and Polezhaev, and Podolinsky, and Myatlev, and Kyukhelbeker, and Glinka, and Odoevsky, and Benediktov, etc. It is the same later also: alongside Nekrasov stands Fet, witnessing by his creative work that Nekrasov alone does not form the epoch and that beside Nekrasov's method there is another one, which it is ture, is not fated to become the main, the pre-eminent one within the limits of its own epoch.

The sharp historical break separating the 30s from the 20s is felt already in Pushkin's creative work. People of the 40s, looking back at the recent

11

past of Russian poetry, clearly felt its *historical* sense. Aksakov, who himself had experienced the force of this upheaval, speaks about it very clearly:[1] "Poetic activity in Russia had to reach the limit of its tension, to develop its apogee. For this the highest poetic genius was necessary and an entire throng of poetic talents. It may appear strange why the setting down of speech in a particular meter and the binding of it with assonances becomes, for certain persons in a given epoch, an irresistible attraction from childhood on. The history of all the arts gives an answer to this question by analogy. In general, when in the spiritual organism of a people the need arises to manifest some special force, then, in order to serve this force, in some inscrutable way people are born into the world with a single common calling. However, they maintain all the diversity of the human personality, preserving its freedom and all the visible, external, accidental qualities of existence. Poetic creativity in its new (for us) measured speech was fated to arise in Russia at a historical turn: and so, you see, at the appointed hour, literally by a mysterious hand, the seeds of the necessary talent are scattered in the wind. They fall haphazardly, now on the Molchanovka in Moscow, on the head of the son of the Guard Captain-Lieutenant Pushkin, who consequently is born with an apparently unnatural inclination for rhymes, trochees, and iambs; now in the Tambov village of Mara on the head of some Baratynsky, now in the Bryansk backwoods on Tyutchev, whose mother and father never even attempted to delight their son with the sound of Russian poetry. It is evident that in these poets, as well as in others contemporaneous to them, unconsciously even for themselves, verse creation was the fulfillment not only of their personal but also of the historical summons of the epoch....Their verse form breathes with a freshness that does not and could not exist in the verse creations of a later period; the fresh trace of victory gained over the material of the word still lies on their verse form; the exultation and joy of artistic possession is still heard. Their poetry and their very relationship to it is stamped with *sincerity*. Lermontov stands on the threshold of this period of sincerity in our poetry. Through the direct force of talent he is affiliated with this brilliant constellation of poets, though remaining detached. His poetry is set off sharply from theirs by the negative character of its content. We see something similar in Heine (although we are not thinking of comparing them), who completed a cycle of German poets. Only one step separates a negative tendency from that tendentious point at which poetry turns into a means and recedes to the background. It has all but been taken. It seems to us that the imprint of this *historical necessity* and sincerity no longer lies on the verse of our time, because to our mind the very historical mission of verse creation has been concluded." As we see, Aksakov sensed the movement of Russian poetry precisely

12

as a *historical process* possessing its own dynamics and not conditioned by the psychic attributes of authors. He feels Lermontov's appearance is foreordained a historically necessary fact prepared by the previous movement of poetry. The creation of new artistic forms is not an act of invention, but one of discovery, because these forms exist latently in the forms of preceding periods. To Lermontov fell the task of discovering that poetic style which had to appear to provide a way out of the poetic impasse created after the 20s and which already existed potentially among some poets of the Pushkin epoch. He had to pass through a complex period of school work in order to orient himself amidst the material accumulated and the methods developed to find a historically-actual path. Between the Pushkin and Nekrasov-Fet epochs a poetry had to be created which, while not breaking with the traditions and achievements of the previous epoch, at the same time would be something distinct from the style which had reigned in the 20s. The time had not yet arrived for a revolution, but the necessity of reform already was sensed very clearly. One had to know how to discard what had become obsolete, and to bring together what was left that still had not lost its vitality, notwithstanding certain inner contradictions occasioned by the struggle of various traditions. It was necessary to blend genres, to invest the poetic line with special emotional intensity, to weight it with thought, to impart to poetry the character of an eloquent, passionate confession, even if as a result of this the strictness of style and of composition suffered. An ornamental airiness of form ("silliness" in Pushkin's words) among the epigones degenerated into a monotonous pattern which repeated itself mechanically and was therefore no longer sensed. A crowd of poets appeared but "no one was listening to poetry when everyone started to write it" (Marlinsky, in the article "On the Novels of N. Polevoy," 1833).

Essentially Lermontov's course was not new; the same traditions remained and the basic principles characteristic for Russian poetry of the 20s underwent only slight modification. Lermontov was a direct disciple of this epoch and did not repudiate it in his creative work, as Nekrasov later did. He appeared at the moment of its decline, when the struggle between the various poetic tendencies had cooled down and a need for reconciliation and summation of results was felt. The struggle of the archaists with Pushkin and Zhukovsky, the quarrels about the ode and the elegy--none of this touched Lermontov. Having skirted this party struggle, which had developed toward the mid-20s and had given rise to Tyutchev's poetry along with Pushkin's, Lermontov weakened those formal problems which disturbed the poets of the older generation (mainly problems of lexicon and genre). He concentrated his attention on other things: on intensifying the expressive energy of the verse line, on imparting an emotional-personal character to poetry, on developing poetic eloquence. Poetry took the form of a lyrical monologue; the verse line once more was motivated as an expression of psychic and intellectual ferment, as a natural expressive means.

The period of high verse culture was ending; poetry had to gain for itself a new reader, one who would demand "rich content." Belinsky, who stood at the head of these new readers, in a contradistinction to other critics (Vyazemsky, Polevoy, Shevyryov) who represented literature, hailed Lermontov as a poet capable of meeting this demand. For him it was important that profound "content" had been introduced into poetry by Lermontov, something which was not to be found in Pushkin, but at the same time Pushkin had not been repudiated. "As the creator of Russian poetry Pushkin eternally will remain the teacher (maestro) of all future poets; but if any one of them, like Pushkin, should be concerned only with the idea of artistry, this would be clear proof of a lack of genius or greatness of talent....Pushkin's pathos lies in the sphere of art itself; Lermontov's pathos lies in the moral problems of fate and the rights of the human personality....The poetic line for Lermontov was only a means for the expression of his ideas, profound and at the same time simple in their merciless truth, and he did not set too much store by it." (*Otechestvennye zapiski,* 1843, No. 2). In a letter to Botkin, Belinsky expresses his view of Lermontov even more definitely: "Lermontov is much inferior to Pushkin in artistry and virtuosity, in the musicality, elasticity, and versatility of his verse line; he yields even to Maykov in all this; but the content of his verse, drawn from the depths of a profound and powerful nature, the gigantic sweep, the demonic flight...--all this compels one to think that in Lermontov we were deprived of a poet who, in terms of content, would have progressed further than Pushkin." *("Pisma" V. G. Belinskogo,* vol. II, p. 284). While not resolving to renounce the past and still preserving complete respect for Pushkin, nevertheless Belinsky already is raising his hand against the "idea of artistry" and beginning to speak about "content" as something special and more important than Pushkin's "artistry." From this it is only one step to the situation which arose in the 60s when only Nekrasov was permitted to write poetry, if, after all, he was unable to express his thoughts in any other way, while Pushkin was ridiculed and discarded as mere verbiage. Lermontov stands on the boundary of these two epochs: while himself bringing the Pushkin epoch to a close, at the same time he is preparing an onslaught against it.

Belinsky's judgment is characteristic for readers of his time. Belinsky is unable to say anything concrete about Lermontov's poetry, as well as about other literary phenomena. In these instances, as a typical reader, he speaks about Lermontov's verse in general phrases and vague metaphors ("a crack of thunder," "a flash of lightning," "the slash of a sword," "the whine of a bullet"). Much more interesting and valuable as material for a concrete, literary-historical study of Lermontov are the judgements of other critics from the writers' camp. Their opinions are notable for far greater restraint: Lermontov's poetry does not produce upon them the impression of a new course. They find "eclecticism" and imitativeness in him; they reproach him for prolixity and vagueness. Only the critic for the *Severnaya pchela*, V. Mezhevich, is close to Belinsky's opinion. In his article the decline in interest in poetry and verse-creation itself is emphasized (speaking about an 1840 anthology of Lermontov's work): "This is such a precious gift for our time, which has become almost unaccustomed to truly artistic works that it really is impossible to admire sufficiently this unexpected find....One must possess a great deal of strength, uniqueness, and originality in order to rivet general attention to *poetry* at a time when verse has lost all of its credit and has been abandoned *to the amusement of children" (Severnaia pchela,* 1840, Nos. 284-285, signature L. L.). Shevyryov understood Lermontov's creative work differently. As a subtle critic and poet groping after new methods beyond Pushkin and standing on the same path as Tyutchev, his opinion is extremely important, the more so since it is distinguished by its sharp definition and concreteness. Shevyryov notes in Lermontov "an uncommon Proteanism of talent, truly remarkable, but nonetheless dangerous to original development ...you hear in turn the sounds of Zhukovsky, Pushkin, Kirsha Danilov, and Benediktov. Even the form of their works is noticeable in everything, and not only in the sounds. Sometimes Baratynsky's and Denis Davydov's phrases flash by; sometimes the manner of foreign poets is evident. And through all this outside influence it is difficult for us to ascertain what properly belongs to the new poet and where he himself stands....Does not the new poet appear to us as some kind of eclectic, who like a bee gathers to himself all the former sweets of the Russian muse in order to create from them new honeycombs? Eclecticism of this kind has occurred in the history of art after its well-known periods: it could also recur among us in accord with the unity of its laws of ubiquitous development....As a poet Lermontov initially appeared as a Proteus with an uncommon talent: his lyre still had not revealed its special pitch; he brings it to the lyres of our best-known poets and with great art is able to tune it to an already well known pitch....We hear the echoes of the lyres already familiar to us and read them as reminiscences of Russian poetry of the last twenty years" *(Moskvitianin,* 1841, pt. II, No. 4, pp. 525-40). In Shevyryov's opinion "a certain personality peculiar to the poet" is revealed in some of Lermontov's poems ("The Gifts of the Terek," "Cossack Cradle Song," "Three Palms," "To the Memory of A.I.

O-yi," "A Prayer"), but "not so much in the poetic form of expression as in the mode of thoughts and in the feelings given to it by life." Such things as "It is both boring and sad," "The Journalist, Reader and Writer,"and "A Meditation" produce a "distressing impression" upon Shevyryov due not to the shortcomings of the verse or the style, but again because of the thoughts and feelings contained in them: "Poet! If indeed such thoughts visit you, it would be better to keep them to yourself and not entrust them to carping society....It seems to us that faithful fragments from real life accompanied by an apathy of observation are unseemly for Russian poetry, and even less so are dreams of despairing disappointment flowing from nowhere." Shevyryov defends high poetry: "a poetry of inspired insights, a poetry of creative fantasy rising above everything essential." In Shevyryov's last reproaches his party position is revealed, but he correctly sensed the presence of a threat in Lermontov's poetry.

Vyazemsky wrote Shevyryov concerning this article (on the 22nd of September, 1841, that is, already after the death of Lermontov): "Apropos of Lermontov. You were too severe with him. Granted, recollections and borrowed impressions are reflected in his talent; but there was also a great deal that signified a strong and fundamental originality which subsequently would have overcome everything external and borrowed. A wild poet, that is, an ignoramus like Derzhavin, for example, could be original from the outset; but a young poet, educated by any learning, upbringing, and reading whatever, inevitably must make his way along well-trodden paths and through a series of favorites who awakened, evoked, and,so to say, equipped his talent. In poetry, as in painting, there must be schools" *(Russkii arkhiv,* 1885, Book 2, p. 307). In essence Vyazemsky does not object to Shevyryov's basic thesis, but only softens its severity and this, seemingly, only under the fresh impression of Lermontov's tragic death. Later (in 1847, in the article "A Survey of Our Literature During the Decade after Pushkin's Death"), Vyazemsky expressed himself on Lermontov even moreseverely and decisively than Shevyryov: "Lermontov had a great gift, but he did not have time to develop himself fully and perhaps couldn't have. To the end Lermontov adhered to the poetic devices for which Pushkin had been celebrated at the beginning of his own career and by which he drew after him the ever impressionable and frivolous crowd. He did not go forward. His lyre did not resound with new strings. His poetic horizon did not expand. An entire, living world is reflected in Pushkin's creations. In Lermontov's works a theatrical world vividly stands out before you with its wings and prompter, who sits in his booth and prompts a speech euphoniously and fascinatingly repeated by a masterly artist" *(Polnoe sobranie sochinenii,*

II, pp. 358-59).

Not to Shevyryov alone belongs the feeling that Lermontov's poetry is eclectic ("recollections of Russian poetry of the last twenty years"), that it had absorbed various, even contradictory, styles and genres struggling against one another. As early as 1824, speaking out against Zhukovsky's poetry *(Mnemozina,* part II) and defending the rights of "high" poetry, Kyukhelbeker expresses himself in the same vein, acknowledging only that the very process of collecting or fusing heterogeneous poetic tendencies is a serious and historically-necessary matter. In his diary for 1844 he notes: "Question: can the talent of an eclectically imitative writer, such as Lermontov is in the greater part of his pieces, rise to the point of originality? The simple or even best imitator of a great or simply gifted poet, of course, would have done better had he never taken pen in hand. But Lermontov is not such a person; he imitates or, rather, one finds in him echoes of Shakespeare, Schiller, Byron, Zhukovsky, and Kyukhelbeker....But in his very imitations there is something of his own, if only the ability to fuse the most heterogeneous verses into a harmonious whole. And this is not a trifle"[2] *(Russkaia starina* 1891, Vol. 72, Book X, pp. 99-100). Kyukhelbeker, who by this time already had withdrawn from direct participation in the literary struggle, apparently himself tended toward the thought of reconciling the parties and saw in Lermontov the possibility of such a reconciliation. Belinsky, too, expresses this same thought, saying that "we see already the beginning of a genuine (not joking) reconciliation of all tastes and all literary parties in the case of Lermontov's compositions." The special emphasis which Belinsky gives to the words "not joking" indicates that a need for reconciliation was sensed and stated even earlier; Lermontov's unique "eclecticism" arose in fulfillment of this need because it represented not a simple aping of one tendency but something different. Shevyryov turned out to be Lermontov's most severe judge precisely because he continued to occupy a militant position and did not strive for "reconciliation." The struggle of the ode and the elegy [3] had to lead to the disintegration of both these genres and, on the one hand, resulted in the lyrics of Tyutchev where the ode, while preserving its oratorical pathos, was condensed and transformed into a lyrical "fragment"(Tynyanov). On the other hand, this disintegration led to the poetry of Lermontov, where the elegy lost its airy classical features and appeared in the form of a declamatory meditation or "reflection." The admirers of strict lyrical genres, like Shevyryov, most acutely felt the instability and fluidity of this form. Gogol, in whose mouth "finished form" (окончанность) or "definitiveness" (окончательность) were the highest form of praise (see, for example, "The Portrait") also sided with him. He does not see this "finality" of form in

Lermontov's creative work and explains this by the absence of love and respect for his own talent: "No one has played so frivolously with his talent, and no one has tried so hard to display an even boastful contempt toward it as Lermontov. Not one poem has gestated full term in him, has been lovingly and thoughtfully fussed over like one's own child, has "settled" and become concentrated in itself; the verse line itself still has not acquired its own firm personality and palely recalls now Zhukovsky's verse and now Pushkin's; everywhere there is excess and prolixity. There is much greater merit in his prose works. Among us no one has written such correct, fragrant prose."

All the judgements cited clearly show that for Lermontov's contemporaries there was nothing unexpected or mysterious in creative work; on the contrary, many of them hailed him precisely because they saw in him the fulfillment of their desires and aspirations. The struggle, of course, had not ended. Belinsky indicates that of all Lermontov's pieces the poem "It's both boring and sad" "attracted the special hostility of the old generation." As we have seen, precisely this piece among others produced a "distressing impression" upon Shevyryov, and provoked a long tirade as to what Russian poetry ought to be like. It is not just a matter of generations here. Shevyryov correctly perceived in these poems of Lermontov the beginning of a course leading to a lowering of the high lyric and to the triumph of verse as an emotional "means of expression" over verse as a self-sufficient, ornamental form. As an archaist and fighter for "a poetry of inspired insights," he did not wish to yield first place to a poetry reduced to the level of an album meditation or to the topical publicistic essay. He was obliged to yield, for precisely that kind of poetry was victorious and became predominant for a time. But "high" lyric poetry, of course, not only did not disappear in Lermontov's time, but even in Nekrasov's time--only the interrelation of these styles changed, which exist and more or less bitterly struggle with one another in every epoch. Nekrasov displaced Fet, but later, in turn, Balmont, Bryusov, and V. Ivanov appeared, and the Nekrasov principle modestly found refuge in "The Satyricon" ("Sasha Chyorny" and others) in order later to blare forth with new strength in the verse of Mayakovsky.[4] A prevailing tendency does not in itself exhaust an epoch and taken in isolation characterizes not so much the state of poetry as readers' sensibilities. In reality the movement of art always is expressed in the form of a struggle for co-existing tendencies. Every literary year accommodates within itself works of various styles. The victory of one of them is a result of this struggle and at the moment of its complete expression is no longer typical for the epoch because behind this victor stand new conspirators whose ideas recently seemed antiquated and worn-out. Every epoch is characterized by a struggle between at least two tendencies or schools (in

18

fact, many more) of which one, gradually triumphing and thereby transforming itself from a revolutionary to a peaceably ruling tendency, becomes encrusted with epigones and begins to degenerate, and another, inspired by a rebirth of old traditions, begins anew to attract attention to itself. At the moment of the disintegration of the first, yet a third tendency usually is formed which attempts to occupy a middle position and, demanding reform, attempts to preserve the main achievements of the victor without condemning itself to an inevitable fall. On the secondary paths, fulfilling temporarily the role of reserves, tendencies remain which do not possess sharply expressed theoretical principles while in practice they develop non-canonized, little-used traditions and, since they are not distinguished by a definiteness of style and genres, work out new literary material.[5]

I return to Lermontov in order to conclude this introductory chapter. "It's both boring and sad" must have disturbed Shevyryov because here the elegy had sunk to the level of a "keepsake" meditation. There is a "low" conversational-melancholic intonation ("Desires!... what's the use of eternally and vainly desiring?... To love... but whom?") and a prosaic phraseology ("it's not worth the effort," "and when you look at life"), which threatened the high lyrical style with such consequences as the poetry of Nadson. On the other hand, it is only one step from "A Meditation" and "The Journalist" to the poetry of Nekrasov. But all the same Lermontov himself does not take this step, remaining on the boundary of two epochs and not breaking with the traditions which formed the Pushkin epoch. He does not create new genres, but on the other hand unhurriedly moves from one to another, blending and smoothing out their traditional particularities. Lyric verse becomes "prolix" and takes the most diverse forms from album notes to ballads and declamatory "reflections"; the poema, so advanced by Pushkin in descriptive and narrative portions, is shortened, acquiring a conventionally decorative character and developing its monologic portion. The genre becomes unstable, but then emotional formulae acquire an extraordinary strength and keenness, which, as will be seen further on, Lermontov carries over from one piece to another without paying attention to distinctions of styles and genres. While not permitting the publication of verses written earlier than 1836, at the same time he constantly employs ready-made formulae coined as early as the period 1830-31. His attention is directed not toward the creation of new material, but to the fusion of ready-made elements.[6] Put somewhat differently, in Lermontov's poetry there is no genuine, organic *constructiveness* in which the material and the composition, mutually influencing one another, make up the form; this is replaced by a tense lyricism and emotional eloquence which is expressed in fixed verbal formulae. All Lermontovian forms tend equally

19

toward their formation, linking the lyric with the poema, the poema with the story (*povest'*), the story with the drama. This, of course, is not a peculiarity of his soul, of his temperament, or, finally, of his individual "verbal consciousness" but an historical fact characteristic of him as an historical individuality who was fulfilling a specific mission required by history. Therefore, neither here nor elsewhere in this book should my words be understood as a simple aesthetic evaluation. This is not an aesthetic but a literary-historical evaluation, whose basic spirit is an enthusiasm for the assertion of fact.

With this I conclude the general description of Lermontov's poetry and turn to the basic questions of his poetics.

CHAPTER I: YOUTHFUL VERSE

1

In the publishing history of Lermontov's works there are certain unique features on which we first of all must dwell.

Lermontov's *Complete Collection of Works* was compiled only by 1891, for the fiftieth anniversary of his death, that is, at a time when the epoch which had formed him had receded into the past. For the readers of the 30s and 40s Lermontov was the author of the novel *A Hero of Our Time* and 70 - 80 poems (only 42 poems were published during his lifetime). In addition, if one takes into account that a poet's influence becomes firmly established mainly through the publication of separate collections, then one must add that besides *A Hero of Our Time* (editions of 1840, 1841, and 1843) Lermontov succeeded in publishing only one collection (1840) of 28 poems (including "The Song of the Merchant Kalashnikov" and "The Novice"). The first posthumous edition of Lermontov's poetry was published in 1842; besides the already well-known works, the drama *Masquerade* was first published here. In the course of 1842-1844 were published several of the last poems of 1841 ("The Dream," "Tamara," "The Prophet," "The Rendezvous," and others) and several early verses (including the narrative poems "The Boyar Orsha" and "Izmail-Bei"). The publication of early works increased in 1859, when a new collection was being prepared (1860, under the editorship of S. Dudyshkin), and especially in 1889 (P. Viskovatov and I. Boldakov).

Lermontov himself did not include a single poem written prior to 1836 in his 1840 collection. Among the works published by him in magazines and almanacs only one, "Angel," dates from an earlier period (1831), but it was not included in the collection. Evidently the year 1836 was sensed by Lermontov himself to be a watershed; he did not consider it possible to print the poems of earlier years. Further, it must be noted that the years 1833-1835 were very meagre creatively, especially in terms of lyric poetry; this is the period of "Junker" verse. Thus, Lermontov's creative work naturally divides into two periods, the school period (1828-1832), and the mature period (1835-1841). Between these two lies an interval of three years when Lermontov is writing very little and is not seriously occupied with creative work. The verse of the first period was unknown to Lermontov's contemporaries, so that

21

the judgements of Shevyryov, Vyazemsky and others cited above are based only on the material of the second period. If Lermontov's youthful, manuscript notebooks had not been preserved, we would know only 40-50 poems and *A Hero of Our Time* as well, instead of the more than 400 poems which now are included in his complete works. To these one must further add the dramas and short stories ("Vadim," "Princess Ligovskaia" and fragments). We would have begun the study of Lermontov with the narrative poem" Khadzhi-Abrek" (his first printed work, which appeared in the *Biblioteka dlia chteniia* for 1835) and with "Borodino" (1837). Of course the study of Lermontov's artistic development would have been greatly hampered, but his literary-historical portrait probably would have acquired more distinct outlines because it would not have have been complicated by the enormous material of the school years, which researchers have not known how to analyze until now.

The posthumous publication of Lermontov's youthful verse made some contemporaries indignant as a violation of authorial wishes, and the question of the appropriate composition and order of an edition of his works long served as a subject of heated arguments. Senkovsky indignantly comes down on the publishers of the 1842 collection, calling them *Herostrati*: "I do not know how else to designate those who, for the sake of profit, are violating the last wish of a talent just deceased, his literary testament....This testament is the collection of his verse published by him prior to his death....He included in it everything from his first attempts that he considered worthy of himself and the readers. He sensibly consigned the rest to oblivion. By what right, when he scarcely had closed his eyes, does profiteering immediately wrench from oblivion all these unsuccessful, unacknowledged first attempts of his pen, mix them with good and acknowledged compositions, compile a tasteless porridge of this mix and publish it in three notebooks or, as they say in the high booksellers' style, in three *parts?*" With respect to the appearance of *Masquerade* in print he indignantly says: "Consequently I will use without permission everything that you are concealing; with a knife I shall scrape out all the journals, all the briefcases, all the tables, and I shall traffic not only in your literary sins but in your love notes and your laundresses' accounts" *(Biblioteka dlia chteniia,* 1843, Vol. LVI, part 2, pp. 39-46). True, such a harsh opinion was expressed by Senkovsky alone, who generally was well known for his sceptical attitude toward contemporary poetry;[7] but the difference beween Lermontov's youthful and later verse troubled many and forced them to vacillate in their opinions. The *Literaturnaya gazeta* for 1843 (No. 9) writes concerning this same 1842 edition: "Of course, from the very first, one is strangely and even unpleasantly struck by the fact that in a book entitled *Poems,* among which are the poet's most beautiful creations in thought and execution, there are several mediocre and inconsistent pieces scant in thought and feelings, and that such a drama as *Masquerade* has been included; but, having reflected thoroughly, one agrees that it could not have been otherwise."

Even Belinsky, who hailed the appearance of everything that it was possible to find, expresses the desire "to see Lermontov's works published quickly in condensed form in two books, the first of which would contain *A Hero of Our Time*, and the other, poems arranged in such an order that the best pieces would be placed consecutively in order of their appearance; after them would follow excerpts from "Demon," "The Boyar Orsha," "Khadzhi-Abrek," *Masquerade*, "The Paymaster's Wife," "Izmail-Bei," and at the end all the slight pieces of lowest merit" *(Otechestvennye zapiski*, 1844, Vol. XXXVII, No. 11).[8]

Lermontov's lycee verse occupies such a large extent that quantitatively it outweighs the creative work of the last years. He begins to write very early (14 years of age) and writes a great deal during the first years. In the first period, 1828-1832, up to 200 verse pieces were written, whereas in the second period, 1836-1841, there were only about 100. During the years 1833-1835 he wrote only 13 poems, among which playful verses and pornographic verse tales ("The Hospital," the "Petergof Holiday," "The Uhlan's Wife") occupy the main place.

From the very beginning Lermontov reveals an attraction to the narrative poem *(poema)* as the most popular and developed genre at this time. In 1828 three narrative poems already had been written: "The Circassians," "The Prisoner of the Caucasus," and "The Corsair"; in 1829 three more: "The Criminal," "Oleg" (a draft in the style of Ryleev's historical "Meditations"), and "Two Brothers"; five in 1830: "Two Slaves," "Dzhulio," "The Lithuanian Woman," "A Confession," "The Last Son of Freedom"; in 1831 four: "Azrail," "The Angel of Death," "Kally," "Aul Bastundzhi." Here in primitive form is revealed that Lermontovian "protaeism" or "eclecticism," which Shevyryov and Kyukhelbeker spoke about. These narrative poems are a unique exercise in the pasting together of ready-made bits and pieces. Lermontov takes the verses of Dmitriev, Batyushkov, Zhukovsky, Kozlov, Marlinsky, Pushkin, even Lomonosov, and creates a certain amalgam *(splav)* from them. Thus, in "The Circassians," lines 16-23 are taken from Dmitriev ("The Crank"); lines 103-112, from Kozlov ("Natalya Dolgorukaya"), as are lines 132-138; the entire ninth (IX) stanza, from Dmitriev ("Moscow Liberated"); the tenth (X) stanza is made up of a combination of Batyushkov ("The Warrior's Dream") and Dmitriev ("Ermak"); and in the intervals lines from Zhukovsky and Pushkin are glimpsed fleetingly.[9]

Sometimes the texts literally coincide, sometimes revisions are made; the text of the original is extended by interpolations or is scattered in various places. As an example, let us compare the ninth stanza of "The Circassians" with Dmitriev's "The Liberation of Moscow" [sic]. (Lermontov's text is on the left):

Начальник всем полкам велел
Сбираться к бою. Зазвенел
Набатный колокол. Толпятся,

Мятутся, строятся, делятся-
Ворота крепости сперлись.
Иные вихрем понеслись
Остановить черкесску силу
Иль с славою вкусить могилу.
И видно зарево кругом.
Черкесы поле покрывают,
Ряды как львы перебегают;
Со звоном сшибся меч с мечем,
И разом храброго не стало.
Ядро во мраке прожужжало,-
И целый ряд бесстрашных пал,
Но все смешалось в дыме чер-
        ном.
Здесь бурный конь с копьем
        вонзенным,
Сквозь русские ряды несется,
Вскочивши на дыбы, заржал,
Упал на землю, сильно рвется,
Покрывши всадника собой.
Повсюду слышен стон и вой.

Вдруг стогны ратными сперлись-
Мятутся, строятся, делятся,
У врат, бойниц, вкруг стен
        толпятся;
Другие вихрем понеслись
Славянам и громам на встречу.
И се - зрю зарево кругом,
В дыму и в пламе страшну сечу!
Со звоном сшибся щит с щитом -
И разом сильного не стало!
Ядро во мраке зажужжало,
И целый ряд бесстрашных пал!
Там вождь добычею Эреве;
Здесь бурный конь, с копьем во
        чреве,
Вскочивши на дыбы, заржал,
И навзничь грянулся на землю,
Покрывши всадника собой;
Отсюду треск и громы внемлю,
Глушащи скрежет, стон и вой.

The commander ordered all the regiments
To prepare for battle. The
Tocsin began to ring. *They throng,*
They are excited, they form up, they
        divide up;
The gates of the fortress are *pressed open.*
Some *rush off like a whirlwind*
To stop the circassian forces
Or to savor the grave with praise
And *all around the glow of battle* is visible.

Suddenly the squares are thronging with
        warriors-
They are excited, forming up, dividing up,
At the gates, the embrasures, around the
        walls they throng;
Others rushed off like a whirlwind
To meet the Slavs and thunderbolts
And lo, I see the glow all around
The fearful battle in the smoke and flame!
Shield resoundingly clashes with shield-

The Circassians cover the field,
Like Lions they overrun our ranks
Sword *resoundingly clashes* with sword
And with one stroke a brave *is no more*
A shell drones in the darkness,
And an entire rank of fearless men falls,
But everything was confused in the black
smoke.
Here an impetuous steed pierced *with a*
lance
Having reared on its hind legs, neighed,
Rushes through the Russian ranks,
Falls to the earth, straining violently,
Covering the horseman with its body.
Everywhere groans and wails are heard.

And with one stroke a strong one is no
more!
A shell begins to drone in the darkness
And an entire rank of fearless men fall.
There is a leader--prey for Erebus;
Here an impetuous steed with a lance in
its belly,
Rearing on its hind legs, neighed,
And crashed backward to the ground
Covering the horseman with its body.
Everywhere I here crashing and thunder-
ing,
Deafening gnashing, groans and wails.

The nature of the revisions is perfectly clear: Lermontov discards every-
thing that sounds like an archaism ("I sě zriu," "Gromy vnemliu," and so on).
Immediately after these lines a quotation from Batyushkov ("The Warrior's
Dream") follows:

А здесь изрубленный герой
Воззвать к дружине верной
хочет -
И голос замер на устах.
Другой бежит на поле ратном,
Бежит, глотая пыль и прах;
Трикрат сверкнул мечем
булатным,
И в воздухе недвижим меч;
Звеня, падет кольчуга с плеч,
Копье рамена прободает,
И хлещет кровь из них рекой;
Несчастный раны зажимает
Холодной, трепетной рукой;
Еще ружье свое он ищет.
Повсюду стук, и пули свищут,
Повсюду слышен пушек вой.

Несчастный борется с рекой,
Воззвать к дружине верной
хочет,
И голос замер на устах!
Другой бежит на поле ратном,
Бежит, глотая пыль и прах,
Трикрат сверкнул мечем
булатным,
И в воздухе недвижим меч !
Звеня, упали латы с плеч,
Копье рамена прободает,
И хлещет кровь из них рекой;
Несчастный раны зажимает
Холодной, трепетной рукой!
Проснулся он и тщетно ищет
И ран, и вражьего копья.
Но ветр шумит и в роще свищет.

And here the maimed hero

The unfortunate struggles with a river,

25

Wants to call out to his faithful
     detachment
And his voice dies on his lips.
Another is running on the martial field,
Running, swallowing dust and powder;
Thrice flashed a damask sword
And the sword is motionless in the air;
Ringing, his hauberk falls from his
     shoulders,
A lance punctures his shoulders
And blood gushes from them like a river;
The unfortunate clutches his wounds
With a cold, trembling hand;
Still is he seeking his rifle.
Everywhere there is rattling and bullets
     whistle
Everywhere the wine of cannon is heard.
	Wishing to call to his faithful detach-
	     ment,
	And his voice died on his lips!
	Another is running on the martial field,
	Running, swallowing dust and powder,
	Thrice flashed a damask sword,
	And the sword is motionless in the air!
	Ringing, the armor falls from his
	     shoulders,
	A lance punctures his shoulders,
	And blood gushes from them like a river,
	The unfortunate clutches his wounds,
	With a cold, trembling hand!
	He has awakened and vainly seeks
	Both his wound and the enemy lance.
	But the wind howls and whistles in the
	     grove.

Then follow four lines from Dmitriev ("Ermak") and, after them, again Batyushkov.

In "A Prisoner of the Caucasus" Lermontov uses material from Pushkin ("A Prisoner of the Caucasus," *Evgeny Onegin),* Kozlov ("Natalya Dolgoruka-ya," "The Monk," "The Bride of Abydos") and Marlinsky (the narrative poem "Andrei Pereyaslavsky"). The Pushkinian plot-line is changed: a third person (the father of the Circassian girl) at whose hand the Russian perishes, traditional for this type of narrative poem, is introduced. At the end appear lines from Byron's "The Bride of Abydos" in Kozlov's translation.

In "The Corsair" Pushkin again is united with Kozlov and Marlinsky ("Brother Brigands," "A Prisoner of the Caucasus," "The Fountain of Bakhchisarai," *Evgeny Onegin*); "The Wide Hellespont" is transferred here from "The Bride of Abydos" together with its epithet ("Where the broad, gray Hellespont," etc.). The very method of combining shows that Lermontov already was very well read in the area of Russian poetry at that time, and preserved a great deal in his memory in order to utilize it in his exercises. In three adjacent lines he unites Pushkin's "A Prisoner of the Cauca-sus" and *Evgeny Onegin:*

Узнав неверной жизни цену, В сердцах людей нашед измену,	И знал неверной жизни цену, В сердцах людей нашед измену. (Кавк. пл.)
Утратив жизни лучший цвет Ожесточился я....	Утратя жизни лучший цвет (Евг. Он.)

Having recognized the value of faith-
less life,
Having found treachery in the hearts
of people,
Having wasted the best flower of life,
I became embittered....

And he knew the value of faithless
life
Having found treachery in the hearts
of people.
("A Prisoner of the Caucasus")
Having wasted the best flower of life
(Evgeny Onegin)

It is interesting that in the same narrative poem we find a quote from Lomonosov's ode: "Ode on the Most Joyous Occasion of the Ascension of Elizaveta Petrovna to the Throne" (1746):

Нам в оном ужасе казалось,
Что море в ярости своей
С пределами небес сражалось,
Земля стонала от зыбей;
Что вихри в вихри ударялись,
И тучи с тучами слетались
И устремлялся гром на гром,
И море билось с влажным
дном,
И черна бездна загоралась
Открытой бездною громов.

Нам в оном ужасе казалось,
Что море в ярости своей
С пределами небес сражалось,
Земля стенала от зыбей,
Что вихри в вихри ударялись,
И тучи с тучами спирались,
И устремлялся гром на гром.
И что надуты вод громады
Текли покрыть пространны
грады,
Сравнять хребты гор с влажным
дном.

It appeared to us in that horror
That the sea in its fury
Was struggling with the bounds of the
heavens,
The earth groaned from the swells;
Whirlwind burst against whirlwind,
And stormclouds sailed *against storm-*
clouds
And thunderclap rushed against thunder-
clap,
And the sea fought with the *damp bottom*
And the black abyss was lit up
With the open abyss of thundering

It appeared to us in that horror
That the sea in its fury
Was struggling with the bounds of the
heavens,
The earth groaned from the swells;
Whirlwind burst against whirlwind,
And stormclouds pressed against storm-
clouds,
And thunderclap rushed against thunder-
clap.
And enormous waves swelled up
Overflowing the vast cities,
Levelling the mountain crests with the
damp bottom [of the sea].

In these youthful exercises is manifested Lermontov's penchant for using ready-made material. He does not simply imitate his chosen "favorite" poet, as usually happens in one's school years; rather he takes ready-made excerpts from various sources and forms a new work from them. We will see that later he does the same thing with his own verse, constructing new poems from old bits and pieces. The creation of material anew does not interest him; hence his early attraction toward [existing] literature. By 1830 Russian literature no longer satisfies him; it seems poverty-stricken, not so much as material for reading per se, as from the point of view of its utilization: "Our literature (he notes in 1830) is so barren, that I cannot borrow anything from it." From that point on begins his intensified reading of foreign literature.

In 1830, as E. A. Khvostova (Sushkova) reports in her "Notes," Lermontov "declaimed Pushkin and Lamartine, and was inseparable from the great Byron." The number of his poems greatly increases (57 poems in 1828-1829, 157 in 1830), and his lyric poetry develops. It is also evident from Lermontov's own notes that precisely in this year he began to be captivated by Byron: "when I began to scribble verse in 1828 (in the *pension*) I rewrote and tidied them up instinctively as it were. I still have them now. Recently I read in the life of Byron that he did the same thing, and the similarity astounded me!" "Byron says that early passion signifies a soul which will love the fine arts." "Another similarity with Lord Byron in my life. An old woman in Scotland predicted to his mother that he would be a *great man* and would marry twice. An old woman foretold *the very same* about me to my grandmother in the Caucasus. God grant that this should happen to me, even if I should be just as unhappy as Byron." The reason for Lermontov's special fascination with Byron lay outside literature: for him Byron was the ideal of "the great man." The fascination with Byron's *life* (T. Moore's book) is characteristic of this entire epoch to the same degree as the enthusiasm for the figure of Napoleon and is related to the sphere of intellectual culture as a whole. "Byronism" as a phenomenon of Russian culture going far beyond the limits of literature must be distinguished from the literary influence of Byron and English poetry in general. By Lermontov's time Byron already had become firmly established in Russian poetry through Zhukovsky, Kozlov, Polezhaev, Podolinsky, Pushkin, and others, along with Scott, Moore, Southey, Wordsworth and others. French literature, already sufficiently utilized, yielded its place to English literature, although it soon appeared anew (Lamartine, Hugo, Balzac, Stendhal, and others). On Russian soil all these foreign writers underwent characteristic transformations in connection with local literary traditions and the needs of the epoch. Thus, in the epoch of Karamzin, Sterne was utilized by Russian literature in the tradition of "sentimentalism" and, moreover, almost exclusively as the author of *A Sentimental*

Journey; whereas in our time he has stirred a new interest in himself and again has entered into literature as an "extreme revolutionary of form," as the author of the parodic novel *Tristram Shandy* (V. Shklovsky). Speaking about "influences," we forget that a foreign author by himself cannot form a new "tendency" because each literature develops in its own way, on the basis of its own traditions. Entering into another literature, the foreign author is transformed and gives it not what he generally possesses and what is typical for him in his own literature, but what is demanded from him. One and the same foreign author can serve as material for completely different literary tendencies depending on precisely what is demanded of him. There can be no "influence" in the real sense of the word, because the foreign author is transplanted on foreign soil not at his own desire, but by a summons. The matter is restricted either to the assimilation of a few devices, the need for which was prepared by the native literary movement, or to the borrowing of necessary material. The latter is particularly noticeable when some single problem comes to the fore within the bounds of the literature under study: a problem of genre, of poetic language, etc.; that is, when there is no "school" or "tendencies," but only a groping for possible and necessary transformations.

Byron originally was utilized for the organization of the new Russian narrative poem, which was being transformed from the "heroic" ode as it existed in the 18th century into the lyrical tale. Zhukovsky and Pushkin simultaneously were drawn toward this source,[10] but remained outside of Byron in their lyric poetry because they still did not need him here. Zhukovsky worked mainly on the creation of a new poetic language and that is why he limited himself to translations. Pushkin, on the other hand, was occupied with the construction of the narrative poem and, while borrowing certain compositional devices from Byron,[11] preserved the characteristic features of the Russian tradition, filling his poems with rich descriptive and historical material ("The Prisoner of the Caucasus," whose descriptive portion goes back to Derzhavin and Zhukovsky, "Poltava," "The Bronze Horseman" and others). In the sphere of the narrative poem only a few changes could be made after Pushkin: on the whole the genre was sufficiently defined and could not develop especially. And, in fact, Lermontov does not create a new genre, but only intensifies the lyrical tension of the narrative poem, following, as we shall see later, the Russian tradition already sufficiently outlined (Polezhaev, Kozlov, Podolinsky). More complex for Lermontov was the problem of lyric poetry. The old genres were exhausted; to Lermontov fell the task of mixing them, weakening their classification, and changing the character of the verse line and style. He gradually draws away from Pushkin toward the line of Zhukovsky and his followers. Here Byron together with

29

Lamartine proved useful to Lermontov. The very linking of these names, which prior to Lermontov we find in Polezhaev (for example, the translation of Byron's narrative poem "Oscar of Alva" and a large number of translations from Lamartine), indicates that Byron alone bore no meaning: it is a matter of tendencies of a special type which had taken shape in Russian lyric poetry of the 20s. The lyrical meditation, as it had been developed by Zhukovsky, had to appear in a new guise: with the tension of lyrical emotion, with an intensification of the oratorical, declamatory tendency, with an assimilation of balladic devices. The genre of the ballad as such does not find ample soil for independent development in Russian poetry (because it has no roots either in folklore, as in English poetry, or in the old bookish lyric), but its stylistic and verse-line peculiarities attract the attention of Russian poets because they aid in the transformation of traditional forms.

At first Lermontov's lyric poetry has a purely school character and bears traces of Merzlyakov's lessons; later (in 1829-30) album verse and epigrams occupy a large place in it. The entitling of poems by generic or formal terms is encountered here quite often (romance, madrigal, ballad, stanza, elegy, song), but predominant among them are forms like the romance and the stanza, which are not strict and not bound by special rules.[12] After 1832 titles of this type disappear completely; the poems either do not have any title or are titled by subject. As concerns the ballad, this designation also figures only in the early poems, and later works of this type (such as "Tamara," "The Quarrel," "The Sea Empress")are not called ballads. Evidently this is connected with the general decline of strict forms and genres characteristic for the 30s. Lermontov does not even employ the term "narrative poem" (*poema*), using instead the term *"povest'"* (tale) ("A Circassian *povest'*," "an eastern *povest'*"), evidently on Byron's model of the "tale." Instead of the elegy, the development of which already had become impossible after its victory at the beginning of the 20s, romances and "melodies" appear; the English poets employed the latter term extensively in their national cycles (T. Moore's "Irish Melodies," Byron's "Hebrew Melodies"). Among our poets Podolinsky and later Fet used the term, apparently pointing to a special emphasis upon intonation. Among Lermontov's youthful poems there is a "Russian Melody" (1829), which probably is titled by analogy with Byron. By this time the term "stanzas" already had acquired a very broad sense, designating a lyrical meditation or an address to another person; Kozlov uses it extensively (evidently by way of Byron). On Russian soil none of these terms are associated with a notion of strict form; their appearance and wisdespread usage attest namely to the vagueness of the lyrical genres. The small form (elegy) arrived to take the place of the large form (ode); after the decline of the elegy, the lyrical forms, while remaining small, lost definite generic outlines; Tyutchev possesses no term for his "fragments." A new struggle of the large forms with the small forms begins, which leads to the victory of the Nekrasov odes and narrative poems over Fet's romances. A division into thematic sections with special titles (Fet's "Evening Lights") becomes traditional for lyric collections. The victory of prose is being prepared, which had taken definite shape clearly by the end of the 40s and whose approach is sensed already in Pushkin's creative work[13] and even more strongly in Lermontov.

Lermontov experiences this historical struggle of forms and genres; he feverishly rushes from lyric poetry to the narrative poem, from the narrative poem to the drama, from the drama to the tale and the novel. Besides lyric and narrative poems, in 1830-31 already the dramas *The Spaniards* (in verse), *Menschen und Leidenschaften* and *A Strange Man* were written, and in 1832 the tale "Vadim" (unfinished). Failing to find new lyrical genres (even to the extent that Tyutchev did), Lermontov evidently is not satisfied with verse and tests his strength on prose, in the dramatic and narrative form. Incidentally, the normativeness of this phenomenon, its historical actuality were noted by Belinsky too; he writes in an article on *A Hero of Our Time:* "Lyric poetry and the tale of contemporary life have been united in a single talent. This union of apparently such contrary types of poetry is not a rarity in our time....For the most part the poetry of our time is the novel and the drama....Our poetry was for the most part lyrical only prior to Pushkin. Pushkin only briefly limited himself to lyricism and soon passed on to the narrative poem, and from it to the drama. As the complete representative of the spirit of his time, he likewise made attempts at the novel." Having worked on the first sketches of the narrative poem "Demon" in 1829-31, Lermontov abandoned it for a long time after attempting to write it in iambic pentameter with masculine rhymes (the verse line which he uses especially often in 1830-31) instead of iambic tetrameter; evidently dissatisfied with it even in this form he made the notation: "I wanted to write this narrative poem in verse, but no, it would be better in prose."

Among the genres which the youthful Lermontov employed, "songs" also occupy a special position. Some of them are titled in connection with their rhythmic properties ("The luminous vision of by-gone days," 1829, and "I do not know whether or not I was deceived," 1830); they relate to a type of "romance" and bear no relationship to folklore. The remainder are folkloric, but to different degrees. 'What is that dust flying in the field" is a well known thieves' song simply noted down or rewritten by Lermontov. [14] The song "The white snow falls in flakes" ("A Russian Song" as Lermontov entitles it), even if it has a folklore basis, is in any case highly stylized in the spirit of the ballad; and apparently the song "The Tocsin Moans" is a translation. Lermontov's attraction to folklore occurred, of course, under the influence of literature and not directly. Incidentally, "folk poetry" was one of the literary genres which drew his attention because of the possibilities of rhythmic innovations. By the beginning of the 30s Russian folklore had entered into literature definitively as a special stylistic variety. Lermontov, understanding the importance of this tradition, notes in 1830: "If I should wish to delve into folk poetry, then surely I would not have to seek elsewhere for it other than in Russian songs."

2

The stylistic and verse-line needs of Russian lyric poetry found support in foreign poetry, from which Russian lyric poetry of the time took what it needed. Much that is completely traditional in Byron and even belongs to the peculiarities not of English poetry but of English verse language appeared in Russian poetry as a new form. Such, for example, is the case with the unequal syllabic intervals between verse stresses and with the variations of anacrusis at the beginning of verse lines, likewise with masculine rhymes in iambic tetrameter and pentameter, where the traditional Russian verse line knew only the alternation of feminine and masculine rhymes. In this sense Byron's "The Prisoner of Chillon" or "Mazepa" did not represent anything new, because feminine rhymes in English verse generally are very rare, and Zhukovsky's "The Prisoner of Chillon" was a verse novelty (repeated later in his "Court in the Underground" from Walter Scott [a portion of *Marmion* - tr.], Polezhaev's "The Arrestee," Kozlov's "A Night in Lara's Castle" from Byron, etc.). Here, as in much else, it is not a question of "Byronism." Incidentally, Apollon Grigorev draws attention to the fact that Byron's influence was felt by "natures even completely alien to the gloomy Byronic mood, by timid and reflective natures," such as Zhukovsky and Kozlov. The natural and necessary conclusion to be drawn from this is that "the natures" alone have a very secondary significance and can explain nothing. Proceeding from his notion of "soul," A. Grigorev maintains that "it is impossible to explain the possibility of such a poetic temper (as in Lermontov's poetry) by the influence of Byron's muse alone, by the sole influence of Byronism."

In the entire question of "foreign influences" in Lermontov[15] the very fact of the Russian poet's attraction to foreign sources and the character of this attraction is important. This attraction was a natural result of the fact that after Pushkin Russian poetry could not develop by means of a simple succession. It was necessary either to revive the old 18th-century traditions (which the archaists insisted upon), or to establish firmly certain more vigorous, although essentially different, recent tendencies based in foreign sources. Lermontov follows precisely this path. The attraction to foreign literatures characteristic of the post-Pushkin epoch achieves special strength in Lermontov: besides Byron we find in his creative work traces of a close acquaintanceship with Moore, Scott, Hugo, Lamartine, Chateaubriand, deVigny, Musset, Barbier, Schiller, Heine, Mickiewicz, etc. This quantity of ties alone attests that before us lies not a fact of simple "influence," but a general attraction toward *foreign literatures* in the search for support and assistance. This was historically necessary just as it was necessary for the Russian Symbolists to seek support in the poetry of Baudelaire, Verlaine, Mallarme, Novalis, Poe, etc., though this tendency itself was sufficiently prepared for by Russian poetry and developed on the basis of its own traditions (V. Solov'ev, Tyutchev, Fet, Polonsky, etc.). We have seen how assiduously Lermontov reads Russian poets in 1829 and how he utilizes them in his poems. Evidently the feeling of barrenness lay in an awareness of exhausted resources. The time of crisis, of the breaking of traditions, had not yet arrived; at the very least it was necessary to broaden the literary horizon, to see the foreign in order to recognize one's own. And this is what Lermontov does.

The choice of writers itself is not new; all these names figure in Russian literature even prior to Lermontov. As I already have said, the combination of Lamartine and Byron is characteristic for Polezhaev (he also made translations of Hugo), and we find a simultaneous enthusiasm for Byron and Hugo in Marlinsky.[16] Baratynsky wrote I. Kireevsky about Barbier even in 1832 (in response to his letter): "For the creation of a new poetry what has been lacking was precisely new, sincere convictions, enlightened fanaticism: as I see it this has appeared in Barbier" (*Tatevskii sbornik,* p. 47). What is new is the ability to combine all this: the freedom to use such vast and diverse material is the art of fusion. What in Marlinsky appeared strange, wild, and protruded like something too deliberate, which was striking but unconvincing, appeared motivated and natural in Lermontov. A. Grigorev remarks that "it is impossible to read Marlinsky at the present time because he flashed by like a meteor even in his own epoch: but the very same elements which rage so wildly in "Ammalat-Bek," and in his endlessly drawn - out "Mulla-Nur," can be admired in Lermontov's creations, unified by the mighty, dominating hand of the artist." This *fusing* is Lermontov's basic concern. He takes everything as material and that is why there are so many direct borrowings in him, although on the whole he remains independent.

Lermontov borrows because he needs specific material, which he finds among a large number of foreign authors. These borrowings are so convincing that no "congeniality" is required for proof of their force. Periodically in every literature there arises a need for foreign material, which then begins to pour into the national channel in a broad stream.[17] Thus, at the beginning of the 20th century we experienced an enthusiasm for northern literatures: Ibsen, Bjørnson, Jacobsen, Hamsun, Lägerlof, etc.; all these writers suddenly became popular among us. This happened precisely at the time of the flowering of Symbolism, when Russian poetry already had developed in a new direction but the paths of narrative prose and the drama were altogether uncertain. Prose underwent a crisis and attention was directed toward the West. In Lermontov's epoch Russian poetry experienced just such a crisis, as dozens of critical articles attest. [18]

The rhythmic possibilities of the traditional Russian meters (especially iambic tetrameter, so developed by Pushkin and his contemporaries) are felt to be exhausted. An attraction to new meters or the modification of old ones becomes progressively clearer. Poems with lines of unequal length develop; an enthusiasm for popular verse emerges (Koltsov), for varied forms of the "song," for dactylic rhymes, etc. Within the limits of a single piece meters often change (Polezhaev's "A Wreath for Pushkin's Grave," Podolinsky's "Meditation," and so on), switching from binary (iambic, trochaic) to ternary meters. A. I. Odoevsky, a close friend of Lermontov, stands among the poets who acknowledged the exhausted state of the old meters and strove for the formation of new ones. He writes poetry with dactylic rhymes ("To A. M. Yanushkevich," 1836):

> В странах, где сочны лозы виноградные,
> Где воздух, солнце, сень лесов
> Дарят живые чувства и отрадные,
> И в девах дышит жизнь цветов,
> Ты был! - пронес пытливый посох странника
> Туда, где бьет воклюзский ключ...
>   и т.д.

> In countries where the grape vines are lush
> Where the air, sun, and forest canopy
> Bestow lively and joyous feelings
> And the life of flowers breathes in maidens
> You were [there] ! - The searching staff of a pilgrim
>   passed
> There, where the Vaucluse spring wells up...
>   etc.

Benediktov too sparkles with dactylic rhymes:

> В дни, когда в груди моей чувство развивалося
> Так свежо и молодо,
> И мечтой согретое сердце не сжималося
> От земного холода, -
> В сумраке безвестности за Невой широкою
> Небом сокровенная
> Мне явилась милая, - дева светлоокая,
> Дева незабвенная.

> In the days when in my breast arose a feeling
> So fresh and young,
> And my dream-warmed heart did not shrink
> From earthly cold,
> In the twilight of obscurity beyond the broad Neva,
> Hidden by the sky
> A dear, bright-eyed maiden appeared to me
> An unforgettable maiden..

In another instance Odoevsky combines a binary (trochaic) with a ternary meter (dactyl), at the same time employing dactylic rhymes ("The Marriage of Georgia and the Russian Kingdom," 1838):

> Дева черноглазая! Дева чернобровая!
> Грузия, дочь и зари и огня!
> Страсть и нега томная, прелесть вечно новая
> Дышит в тебе, сожигая меня!

> Black-eyed maiden! Dark-browed maiden!
> Georgia, daughter of dawn and light!
> Passion and voluptuous languor, charm eternally new
> Breathes in you, consuming me!

Then the meters change anew:

> Гордо идет, без щита и меча...
> Только с левого плеча
> Зыблясь падает порфира:
> Светл он как снег, грудь что степь широка,
> А железная рука
> Твердо правит осью мира!

Proudly he goes without shield or sword...
Only the purple falls rippling from his left shoulder:
He is bright as snow, a chest as broad as the steppe,
But an iron hand
Firmly governs the axis of the world!

The literary historical and theoretical basis of these experiments is contained in Odoevsky's well-known article written in regard to the appearance in Russian of Rotrou's tragedy "Venceslas" in A. Zhandr's adaptation (1825). Here Odoevsky praises Zhandr for not using iambic hexameter: "The boldest *vers libre* has taken the place of the strained and inflated iambic hexameter verse line, which none of our poets ever mastered and still have not mastered perfectly. Men of letters gifted with good taste never regarded this measure fitting for tragedy. This poetic form was grafted upon us from the French as the closest approximation of their Alexandrine. The Germans long ago ceased to imitate it and laugh at Gottsched. The English have never imitated it. Alfieri wrote blank verse (sciolti), which indeed are necessary in tragedy for the exposition of powerful feelings in all their naked simplicity." Odoevsky further points to the difference between the French and Russian verse line: "The French also possess this peculiarity: their prosody is syllabic and stresses fall indeterminately. We have six ponderous *iambs* badly replaced by *pyrrhics,* dragging along one after the other and pounding on one's ear like a hammer. Is it really possible that our Russian language, both sonorous and manly, will be confined eternally in this cramped, monotonous casing for the expression of the most ardent impulses: *cramped* not for an isolated happy expression alone, but for a fullness of feelings and an uninterrupted sequence of thoughts. All the known meters, other than the iambic, are too dance-like and uncharacteristic of tragedy, where poetry is clothed in conversational language. Thus, while preserving our usual prosody, one must seek all possible variety....In conclusion let us say that not only those innovations which are well received by general opinion are useful, but the experiments themselves yield a genuine benefit when they tend toward deliverance from excessive bonds unrelated to the laws of nature and art."

Griboedov, too, writes about the same thing in his "Desiderata" (1824 - 1825) (*Akad. Izd.* , III. p. 100): · "Excessive precision in the structuring of poetic feet *(stoposlozhenie)* is useless and is only evident among the French and among us; it does not exist among the English and the Germans, and among the ancients the hexameter proves that there also they did not adhere to it."

In his youthful verse (1830-31) Lermontov also makes certain experiments in the realm of rhythm; this is one of the results of his acquaintance with German and English poetry. In 1830, that is, precisely when he began to be fascinated by Byron, ternary measures with variations of anacrusis and with internal rhymes (a device especially characteristic of the ballad, see Zhukovsky's "The Castle of Smalgolm") appear in his verse, and sometimes even the unequal syllabic intervals between stresses characteristic of contemporary Russian poetry (Blok, Akhmatova, etc.). Prior to Lermontov, verse of this type is encountered from time to time in Zhukovsky, Marlinsky, Podolinsky (never in Pushkin). In the course of 1830-31 Lermontov writes twelve such poems; henceforth he abandons these experiments and returns to classical measures. During the entire second period only one poem of the ballad type, "The Mermaid" (1836), has varying anacruses. The English origin of these experiments is confirmed by such things as a translation of the Byronic ballad from *Don Juan* (1830), where we find all these innovations:

> Берегись! берегись! над бургосским путем
>   Сидит один черный монах;
> Он бормочет молитву во мраке ночном,
>   Панихиду о прошлых годах.
> Когда Мавр пришел в наш родимый дол
>   Оскверняючи церкви порог,
> Он без дальних слов выгнал всех чернецов;
>   Одного только выгнать не мог.[19]

> Beware! Beware! Above the Burgos road
> A black monk *sits* alone.
> He mutters a prayer in the night gloom,
> A requiem for years gone by.
> When the *Moor arrived* in our *native vale*
> Defiling the threshold of the church
> Without *further ado* he drove out all the black monks.
> Only one was he unable to expel.

The rhythmic tendency subordinates everything else to itself; the syntax conforms to it with difficulty: awkward phrases are formed, the verse line does not flow freely, the rhythmic *dominanta* is conspicuous.

> Видали ль когда, как ночная звезда
> В зеркальном заливе блестит;

Как трепещет в струях, как серебряный прах
От нее рассыпаясь бежит.
Но поймать ты не льстись, и ловить не берись,
Обманчивы луч и волна...
Мрак тени твоей только ляжет на ней;
Отойди ж - и заблещет она. -
Светлой радости так беспокойный призрак
Нас манит под хладною мглой;
Ты схватить - он шутя убежит от тебя; —
Ты обманут - он вновь пред тобой.

("Звезда" 1830 г.)

Have you ever seen how the night star
Glitters in the mirroring gulf;
How it trembles in streams, how silver dust
Sprinklingly runs from it.
Do not flatter yourself that you'll capture it and do
                                  not try to,
The ray and the wave are deceptive....
Only the gloom of your shadow will fall on *it*;
Move away and *it* will begin to sparkle.
Thus, the restless phantom of bright joy
Beckons us beneath the cold gloom
You grasp - it playfully flees from you;
You have been deceived - again it is before you.

In Podolinsky's ballads and "melodies" one encounters timid attempts at a similar surmounting of classical meters by means of a variety of anacruses or the violation of the syllabic identity of the intervals between stresses:

Победитель вперед -
Вот и терем с высот
Забелел между башен зубчатых,
Колья вбиты вокруг,
И на них ряд кольчуг
Да черепы в шлемах косматых...

("Девичь-гора")

Уж поздно - и туча легла как свинец,
По Волхову ветер гуляет,
Откликнулся ворон, торопися, пловец -
Недоброе ворон вещает!

("Предвещание")

38

Есть чудная арфа, с колыбели она
До самой могилы играет,
Сокрыта глубоко, не видна, не слышна,
Нигде, никогда не смолкает.

(''Мелодия'')

The conqueror advances -
And from the heights the tower-chamber
Whitened between the castellated turrets,
Stakes are driven in all around,
And on them a row of hauberks
And *skulls* in shaggy helmets....

(''The Virgin Mountain'')

It was already late and a stormcloud lay like lead,
The wind strolls along the Volkhov,
The raven echoed, *hasten,* swimmer ;
The raven does not prophesy welcome news! [nedobroe]

(''The Portent'')

There is a miraculous harp, it plays
From the cradle to the very grave,
Hidden deeply, *invisible,* inaudible,
Nowhere, never does it cease.

(''A Melody'')

Neither Podolinsky nor Lermontov developed their rhythmic experiments to the point that they immediately entered into Russian poetry. It is known that similar rhythmic variations exist in Tyutchev's and Khomyakov's work, but evidently their development, which was still impossible then, has since taken place in our era. These experiments remained as a hint of the possibility of future reform. Russian poetry organically moved toward a simplification of rhythm and the verse line in general: toward a weakening of the dynamic of rhythm. Intonation advances to the forefront either in the form of a melody, as in the romances of Fet and Polonsky, or in the song-couplet of oratorical form, as in Nekrasov.

It is characteristic that along with the rhythmic experiments introducing the English balladic ''pause'' into Russian poetry, we see another process in Lermontov: the breaking down of the classical verse line. Beginning in 1830 we already have the Lermontovian iambic pentameter with free caesurae and masculine rhymes only, which, owing to the enormous quantity of sharp enjambments, creates an impression more of rhythmic prose than poetry. This destruction of the classical iamb concurrently with the development of ternary measures testifies to the fact that the old verse was exhausted. But it also reveals an acquaintance with the English verse line. Even the octave, in which masculine rhymes had to alternate with feminine rhymes in accordance with the tradition strictly preserved by Pushkin ("The House in Kolomna"), appears in a new form in Lermontov with only masculine rhymes ("July 15, 1830," "The Plague," "The Harp"). On Byron's model Lermontov employs the octave also for satire ("The Boulevard"). The year 1830 is especially rich with iambic pentameter of this type: the narrative poems ("Dzhyulio") and "The Lithuanian Woman") are written in it. In 1831 it acquires an especially sharp, prosaic character as in the poem "June II, 1831 ," which goes wholly beyond the bounds of the customary lyric genres and represents a free form of the meditation (like Byron's "Epistle to Augusta," which probably served as a model):

Моя душа, я помню, с детских лет
Чудесного искала. Я любил
Все обольщенья света, но не свет,
В котором я минутами лишь жил;
И те мгновенья были мук полны,
И населял таинственные сны
Я этими мгновеньями. Но сон,
Как мир, не мог быть ими омрачен.

Since childhood years, I recall, my soul
Has sought the marvelous. I have loved
All the temptations of society, but not society,
In which I have lived but moments;
And those moments were filled with torment,
And I peopled secret dreams
With these moments. But a dream,
Like the world, can not be darkened by them.

After 1831 Lermontov completely abandons this iambic in lyric poetry as well as in narrative poems.

In Lermontov's youthful verse another peculiarity already is noticeable, relating to the area of style and connected with the general tendency of Russian poetry of this time toward weighting lyric poetry with thought, with "content," as Belinsky expressed it. Verse formulae begin to take shape which attach special semantic weight to a poem, and stand out boldly against the background of the remaining lines. They are independent in their semantic influence and for that reason exist easily by themselves outside any connection with what precedes or follows. Odoevsky, ill-disposed toward French poetry, made note of this phenomenon (probably thinking of Baratynsky and Vyazemsky) as an undesirable one introducing rationality into poetry: "Many seek not poetry in verse creation but memorable *(za-metnykh)* verse lines; they are enraptured when the poet sacrifices the symmetry of the whole to an individual thought, often brilliant only for its arrangement of ideas and sham moralizing." Especially curious here is the indication that the semantic significance of these "memorable verse lines" is dependent precisely upon the verse form ("arrangement of ideas"). Odoevsky's words date from 1825, when this process still was scarcely noticeable. Lermontov undoubtedly is concerned already for the creation of such "memorable verse lines," and Shevyryov points to them (especially at the ends of poems) as a characteristic feature of some of Lermontov's pieces. He says that the poems "Do not believe yourself," "The First of January," and "Meditation" are sharpened at the end by an idea or comparison and that his manner "recalls Baratynsky's turn of speech, who in many of his poems beautifully expressed in our language what among the French is called *la pointe,* and for which there is no corresponding word in the Russian language" (*Moskvitianin,* 1841, part 4, p. 533). In its essence this oratorical device is linked to Lermontov's general penchant for eloquence. He likes *Werther* more than *La nouvelle Heloise,* but Rousseau possesses an "astonishing eloquence" (notation of 1831). There are a great many such formulae in Lermontov's youthful verse; it is obvious that he cares about them and especially seeks them out:[20]

И целый мир возненавидел,
Чтобы тебя любить сильней.
. . . .
Он тень твоя, но я люблю,
Как тень блаженства, тень твою.
. . . .
Зачем же гибнет все,что мило,
А что жалеет, то живет?
. . . .
Безумцы! Не могли понять,
Что легче плакать, чем страдать
Без всяких признаков страданья!
. . . .
И сном никак не может быть,
Все, в чем хоть искра есть страданья!
. . . .
Когда я свои презираю мученья,
Что мне до страданий чужих?

. . . .
Чья душа слишком пылко любила,
Чтобы мог его мир полюбить.

. . . .
Расстаться казалось нам трудно,
Но встретиться было б трудней!

. . . .
А он, мятежный, просит бури,
Как будто в бурях есть покой!

And I came to hate the entire world,
In order to love you more strongly.
. . . .
[It, he?] is your shadow, but I love
Your shadow, like the shadow of bliss.
. . . .
Why should everything perish that's dear,
And what has regrets, lives?
. . . .
Madmen! They could not understand
That it is easier to cry than to suffer
Without all the signs of suffering!
. . . .
Nowise can everything be a dream
In which there is even a spark of suffering!
. . . .
When I despise my own torments,
What are the sufferings of others to me?
. . . .
Whose soul has loved too ardently,
So that the world might grow fond of him.
. . . .
It seemed difficult for us to part,
But it would be more difficult to meet!
. . . .
And he, the rebellious one, begs a storm
As if there is refuge in storms!

Often a simile plays the role of such *pointes* (there is an abundance of concluding "thuses" [tak] in Lermontov).

Lyric poetry acquires unstable outlines: the "excess and prolixity" noted by Gogol appear. Passages emphasized from a semantic point of view ("memorable verse lines") stand out, in comparison with which everything else has a vague, diffuse character. Upon examining his notebooks Lermontov frequently strikes out a considerable part of a poem written earlier (sometimes an entire half), evidently considering it too drawn out. Shevy-ryov not without reason points up the similarity to Baratynsky. Baratyn-sky's poetry, which often takes the form of lyrical meditations sharpened with aphorisms, in many respects was closer to Lermontov than Pushkin's poetry, which always is balanced and light in its outlines. E. A. Khvostova relates how Lermontov once (in 1834) was conversing with her during the singing of a romance to the words of Pushkin's "I loved you": "When he (Yakovlev) began to sing:

> Я вас любил, любовь еще, быть может,
> В душе моей погасла не совсем, -
>
> (I loved you, and perhaps love still
> Has not been extinguished completely in my soul,),

"Michel" whispered to me that these words clearly expressed his feelings at the present moment.

> Но пусть она вас больше не тревожит,
> Я не хочу печалить вас ничем.
>
> (But let it not trouble you further
> I do not wish to sadden you with anything.)

'O, no,' Lermontov continued in an undertone, 'Let it trouble you - that is the surest means of not being forgotten.'

> Я вас любил безмолвно, безнадежно,
> То робостью, то ревностью томим.
>
> (I loved you silently, hopelessly,
> Tormented now by timidity, now by jealousy.)

'I do not understand timidity and silence,' he whispered, 'and hopelessness I grant to women.'

> Я вас любил так искренно, так нежно,
> Как дай вам бог любимой быть другим.
>
> (I loved you so sincerely, so tenderly,
> As God grant you should be loved by another.)

'That has to be changed completely; is it natural to wish happiness to one's beloved, and particularly with another? No, let her be unhappy. I understand love in such a way that I would prefer her love to her happiness. Were she to be unhappy on my account, that would bind her eternally to me....*All the same it is a pity that I did not write these lines, only I would have changed them somewhat.* However, Baratynsky has a play which I like much more; it even more faithfully depicts my past and present,' and he began to declaim:

Нет, обманула вас молва,
Попрежнему я занят вами.
И надо мной свои права
Вы не утратили с годами.
Другим курил я фимиам,
Но вас носил в святыне сердца,
Другим молился божествам,
Но с беспокойством староверца!

No, rumor has deceived you
I am preoccupied with you as before.
And with the years you have not lost
Your rights over me.
I have burnt incense to others,
But carried you in the temple of my heart,
I have prayed to other divinities,
But with the anxiousness of an Old Believer!

'You, Mikhail Yurevich, have no cause to envy these lines. You have expressed yourself even better':

Так храм оставленный - все храм,
Кумир поверженный - все бог!

Thus the temple abandoned is still a temple,
The idol cast down - still a god!

'You remember my lines? You have preserved them? For God's sake give them to me; I have forgotten some of them. I will rework them for the better and dedicate them to you.' " *(Notes,* pp. 140-141).

Against the background of this conversation on the poems of Pushkin and Baratynsky, one of Lermontov's album poems (1830) acquires a somewhat special meaning: namely the poem whose conclusion Khvostova quotes:

Я не люблю тебя; страстей
И мук умчался прежний сон;
Но образ твой в душе моей
Все жив, хотя бессилен он;
Другим предавшися мечтам,
Я все забыть его не мог; -
Так храм оставленный - все храм,
Кумир поверженный - все бог! -

> I do not love you; the former dream
> Of passions and torments has rushed away;
> But your image in my soul is
> Still alive, though powerless;
> Having given myself up to other dreams,
> Still I could not forget it;
> Thus a temple abandoned is still a temple,
> The idol cast down - still a god!

Here Lermontov indeed is very close to Baratynsky; the difference lies only in that Baratynsky's simple and restrained lyrical theme acquired an intense ("dream of passions and torments") and slightly paradoxical character in Lermontov. In Baratynsky there is an ordinary metaphor (temple of my heart) which is realized and creates the possibility of concluding the poem with an elegant conceit prepared beforehand; in Lermontov there is in place of this an unexpected, emphatic simile making a sharp *pointe*. Lermontov returns to this poem in 1837 and recasts it, preserving, however, the conclusion intact:

Расстались мы, но твой портрет
Я на груди моей храню;
Как бледный призрак лучших лет,
Он душу радует мою.

И новым преданный страстям,
Я разлюбить его не мог:
Так храм оставленный - все храм,
Кумир поверженный - все бог!

> We have parted, but your portrait
> I preserve on my breast;
> Like a pale phantom of better years,
> It gladdens my soul.
>
> And devoted to new passions

I could not cease loving it:
Thus a temple abandoned is still a temple,
An idol cast down - still a god!

The concluding simile, so carefully preserved by Lermontov, is not distinguished by originality; it is in vogue for Chateaubriand (Duchesne, Vogué) and, apparently, not for him alone.[21] Lermontov's verse abounds in borrowings of this type both from Russian and foreign literatures, but this is not evidence of "influence" or "congeniality"; rather it attests to what Shevyryov, Kyukhelbeker, and Gogol all pointed out: that for the most part in Lermontov the poetic *material* is someone else's, and that his main concern lies in combining and fusing it.

Such work based on someone else's materials is characteristic of writers who bring a literary epoch to a close. The acquisition of new material and its initial working-out constitutes the lot of "younger" writers; therefore in their own work they do not achieve particular formal polish. On the other hand, writers canonizing or ending a given period use this material because their attention is concentrated on method. Lermontov's method in this sense is *a priori*: he needs similes and aphorisms and seeks them everywhere. One is justified in suspecting that every simile or maxim of his is borrowed, or at least is modeled on others. One must say generally that similes and metaphors are material which constantly is transferred from one poet to another. This occurs, of course, because, contrary to widely-held opinion, it is not the "image" which comprises the essence of poetic language, but the device of comparison, of *allegory* itself. Often the most refined and complex metaphors, whose invention we are inclined to ascribe exclusively to the imagination of a given poet, in fact take their origin in another poet who probably also found them in a literary source.[22] One might think that by tracing the life of any metaphor step by step, we would arrive at its simplest form, at the everyday verbal metaphor which by itself possesses no "poetic" meaning, and acquires it only when it *aims* at allegory as a stylistic method.

Lermontov specially collects similes in order to use them later, and he uses each of them many times. He notes in 1830: "When I was still small, I loved to look at the moon, at the various clouds which, in the shape of knights in helmets, seemed to crowd around her, as if they were knights full of jealousy and anxiety accompanying Armida into her castle. In the first act of my tragedy, Fernando, talking with his beloved beneath the balcony, speaks about the moon and uses this foregoing simile about the knights." Indeed, we read in *The Spaniards* (Act I, Scene II):

46

Взгляни опять: подобная Армиде,
Под дымкою сребристой мглы ночной,
Она идет в волшебный замок свой.
Вокруг нее и следом тучки
Теснятся, будто рыцари-вожди,
Горящие любовью; и когда
Чело их обращается к прекрасной,
Оно блестит, когда же отвернуто
К соперникам, то ревность и досада
Его нахмурят тотчас - посмотри,
Как шлемы их чернеются, как перья
Колеблются на шлемах...

Look again: like Armida,
Under the silvery haze of the nocturnal darkness
She is going into her enchanted castle,
Around her and after little clouds
Crowd, as if they were knight-chieftains,
Burning with love; and when
Their brow turns to the beautiful one
It shines; but when it turns
To rivals, then jealousy and spite
Immediately furrow it. Look!
How their helmets darken, how feathers
Flutter on the helmets...

Traces of this simile are encountered many times, not only in the youthful but in the mature verse as well ("Aul Bastundzhi," "Izmail-Bei," "Sashka").

E. Khvostova reports that in Desbordes-Valmore's novel *L'Atelier d'un peintre*, Lermontov, incidentally, underscored the phrase "ses yeux remplis d'étoiles" and wrote in the margin "comme les votres - je profiterai de cette comparaison."

The literary sources of many of Lermontov's similes, often extraordinarily refined and complex, are completely clear. In Byron's "The Bride of Abydos" it is said of Jafar's daughter that she is "pure as a prayer on the lips of children" (Kozlov's translation).[23] Lermontov employs this simile in an 1830 draft ("The Blue Mountains of the Caucasus"): "The air is pure there, like a child's prayer." And it occurs in altered form in *A Hero of Our Time* (evidently directly from this draft): "The air is pure and fresh, like a child's kiss."

The youthful verse is saturated with similes which sometimes accumulate like an entire stratum. They serve, of course, not to elucidate the subject at hand, but on the contrary usually draw attention away from the subject. These similes reveal a need for "eloquence," and a lack of interest in description as such (in contrast to Pushkin). Here are some examples of such similes:

Раздвинул тучи месяц золотой,
Как херувим - духов враждебный рой.[24]
Как упованья сладостный привет
От сердца гонит память прошлых бед.

("Литвинка," Х11)

The golden moon parted the clouds
Like a cherub - a hostile swarm of spirits.
As the sweet greeting of hope
Drives the memory of past misfortunes from the heart.

("The Lithuanian Woman,"XII)

На нем пещера есть одна -
Жилище змей - хладна, темна,
Как ум, обманутый мечтами,
Как жизнь, которой цели нет,
Как недосказанный очами
Убийцы хитрого привет.

("Ангел смерти" 1)

There is one cavern in [the hill]
Cold, dark, the dwelling of snakes,
Like a mind deceived by dreams
Like a life which has no aim,
Like the half-spoken greeting
In the eyes of a cunning assassin.

("The Angel of Death," I)

Lermontov's youthful prose ("Vadim") is replete with similes which sometimes are so weakly motivated from the standpoint of the subject that their methodological, *a priori,* and stylistic nature is bared completely: "at these moments his anxious soul, embracing all the past, resembled a criminal condemned by the Spanish Inquisition to fall into the piercing embraces of the *madonna dolorosa,* this perverted, blasphemous, terrible image of the holiest of holies." The members of the simile can be re-arranged: in one

48

instance the glitter of flickering lamps is compared to an idea in a mind crushed by grief; in another, marvelous and gloomy thoughts are compared to a solitary monastery ("A motionless monument to the weakness of certain people"). Thus, in Chateaubriand a tall column standing alone in a desert is compared to a great thought which sometimes arises in a soul ("cette haute colonne qui se montre seule debout dans le désert, comme une grande pensée s'élève par intervalle dans une âme"), and in Lamartine, on the contrary, a solitary thought is compared to a pyramid standing in a desert ("Et puis il s'élevait une seule pensée, Comme une pyramide au milieu des déserts"). A different simile may be employed seriously in one instance, and humorously in another. Thus, the comparison of a heart to an American well at whose bottom a crocodile is hiding, used by Chateaubriand in *Atala*, and which subsequently appeared many times in Russian literature (Batyushkov, Benediktov, even Leskov), is encountered twice in Lermontov. First it appears completely seriously in "Vadim" ("at the bottom of this pleasure sits an inexplicable sadness, like a venomous crocodile in the depths of a pure, limpid American well"), later parodically in "Princess Ligovskaya" ("Such a housemaid, seated at work in the back room of a respectable home, resembles a crocodile at the bottom of a bright American well").

Sometimes Lermontov borrows individual formulae, similes, or expressions directly from Byron. Byron's poem "Lines inscribed: on this day I complete my thirty-sixth year" (1824) begins with the lines:

> T'is time this heart should be unmoved
> Since others it hath ceased to move,

In Lermontov we find:

> Время сердцу быть в покое
> От волненья своего,
> С той минуты как другое
> Уж не бьется для него.
> 1830 г.

> It is time for the heart to be at rest
> From its anxiety.
> From that moment when another [heart]
> No longer beats for it.

In accord with the tradition adopted by Lermontov, this poem concludes with a simile which belongs to Coleridge ("Christabel"), and which was taken by Byron as the epigraph to the poem "Fare thee well," translated by Kozlov:

> Так два расторгнутых грозою,

Утеса мрачные стоят;
Их бездна с ревом разлучает,
И гром разит и потрясает, -
Но в них ни гром, ни вихрь, ни град
Ни летний зной, ни зимний хлад
Следов того не истребили,
Чем некогда друг другу были.

Thus torn by the storm two
Somber crags stand:
A chasm parts them with a roar,
And thunder strikes and shakes,
But in them neither thunder, nor whirlwind, nor hail
Nor the summer's heat, nor winter's cold
Has destroyed the traces of that
Which once they had been to each other.

Lermontov condenses [the passage]:

Так расселись под громами,
Видел я, в единый миг
Пощаженные веками
Два утеса бреговых;
Но приметно сохранила
Знаки каждая скала,
Что природа съединила,
А судьба их развела.

Thus split by lightning bolts
In one instant, I saw,
Two coastal crags
Spared by the ages;
Each crag visibly
Preserved signs [indicating]
That nature had joined,
But fate had sundered them.

This same simile is used once more by Lermontov in the poem "Ro-mance" (1830):

Стояла серая скала на берегу морском;
Однажды на чело ее слетел небесный гром.
И раздвоил ее удар, - и новою тропой

50

Между разрозненных камней течет поток седой.
Вновь двум утесам не сойтись, - но все они хранят
Союза прежнего следы, глубоких трещин ряд.
Так мы с тобой разлучены злословием людским

и т.д.

A grey crag stood on the seashore;
Once a heavenly bolt flew down against its brow
And the blow split it; in a new path
A grey stream flows between the sundered rocks.
The two crags will never be joined anew, yet they
still preserve
Traces of a former bond, a row of deep fissures.
Thus you and I were parted by human calumny.

Traces of this simile are found in "The Novice," but already as an element of description:

Я видел груды темных скал,
Когда поток их разделял,
И думы их я угадал,
Мне было свыше то дано!
Простерты в воздухе давно
Объятья каменные их,
И жаждут встречи каждый миг;
Но дни бегут, бегут года,
Им не сойтиться никогда.

I saw the hulks of dark crags
When a stream was parting them
And I guessed their thoughts
It was granted to me from above!
Long since their stone embraces
Have been raised in the air
Thirsting every instant for a meeting;
But days fly by, and fly the years
Never will they come together.

"Stanzas" (1830) begins with the lines:

Взгляни, как мой спокоен взор,
Хотя звезда судьбы моей
Померкнула с давнишних пор,
И с нею думы светлых дней. -

51

> See, how calm my glance
> Though the star of my fate
> Since ancient times has dimmed,
> And with it thoughts of bright days.

In Byron we find (the beginning of the poem "Stanzas to Augusta"):

> Though the day of my destiny's over,
> And the star of my fate hath declined
>
> etc.

The poem "A Prophecy" (1830) concludes with the lines:

> И будет все ужасно, мрачно в нем,
> Как плащ его с возвышенным челом.

> And all will be terrible, gloomy in it
> Like his cloak with upraised brow.

In the wording of the rough draft of these lines a link with Byron and Kozlov is revealed.

> И будет все ужасно, черно в нем,
> Как длинный плащ с клонящимся пером.

> And all will be terrible, and black in it,
> Like a long cloak with feather trailing.

In Kozlov's translation of a passage from Byron's "Lara" we find:

> Кудрей густых цвет черный, мрак чела
> И зыбкий склон широкого пера.

> The black color of thick curls, a darkness of brow
> And the unsteady arc of a broad quill.

3

If even Lermontov's mature lyric poetry sounded like "reminiscences of Russian poetry of the last two decades" to Shevyryov, Vyazemsky, Kyukhelbeker, and Gogol, then what would they have said about his youthful verse filled with stock poetic phrases taken from Zhukovsky, Pushkin, Kozlov, Marlinsky, Polezhaev, etc.? To later readers, who had forgotten all this material and who retained only the poetry of Pushkin from this entire epoch, it might have seemed that Lermontov was wholly original, unique, and "enigmatic." It is worth immersing ourselves in the lyric poetry of the 20s in order to see the sources of Lermontov's style. One must assume that a great deal will become even clearer when we enlist the mass (journal and almanac) poetry of the time in our study. This is the next task awaiting us, and one which demands for its realization not only a great deal of preparatory work, but the presence of clear theoretical premises and principles as well. Here are several examples which illustrate the traditional character of Lermontov's youthful verse.

In the poetic practice of the 20s we encounter a series of recurring turns of speech and similes, the majority of which originate in Western literature. To their number belong, for example, the comparison of a man to a bark abandoned at sea or cast up on a beach by a storm. In Zhukovsky this simile still retains the form of an allegory (as in Derzhavin's "The Sinking"), whose development forms the content of an entire poem ("The Swimmer," 1811, "Stanzas," 1815). Later the man-bark allegory loses its poetic force, but a fragment of it remains which continues to live. The poet's attention willingly lingers on it even in those instances when it has no symbolic significance. In Byron's "The Bride of Abydos" the dawn after a storm is described: various traces of the storm are visible on the shore, including "A broken torch, an oarless boat." In his translation Kozlov composes two special lines from this reference to a bark:

> Вот опрокинутый челнок
> Волною брошен на песок.

> Here is a capsized bark
> Tossed on the beach by a wave.

Kozlov has a poem "Two Barks" in which we have a developed allegory, as we also have in Zhukovsky: two oarsmen in different boats, one of which is completely in flowers and has a white sail, whereas over the other rises a black sail, symbolize the various fates of man. This simile crops up briefly in various poems by Kozlov:

> Я волн и бурь не устрашился, -
> И в легком челноке моем

53

Отважно по морю пустился

        ("К другу В. А. Жуковскому")

I was not frightened by the storms and waves
And in my light bark
I bravely set off across the sea
        ("To a Friend, V. A. Zhukovsky")

Привлек ты к пристане надежной
Разбитый челн грозой мятежной.

        ("Наталья Долгорукая")

You drew to a safe haven
A bark broken by the rebellious storm.
        ("Natalya Dolgorukaya")

Как ветер ни гонит мой бедный челнок
   Пучиною жизни мятежной,
Где я так уныло и так одинок
   Скитаюсь во тьме безнадежной...

        ("Графине З. И. Лебцельтерн"

          из А. Шенье

No matter how the wind drives my poor bark,
By the maelstrom of a restless life,
Where I so wearily and so solitary
Wander in despairing darkness...
        ("To the Countess Z. I. Lebzeltern,"
          from A. Chénier.)

Further in Polezhaev:

Оставлен всеми, одинок,
Как в море брошенный челнок
В добычу яростной волне.

. . . .

Давно челнок мой одинокий
Скользит по яростной волне

. . . .

Темнеет ночь, гроза бушует,
Несется быстро мой челнок.

Abandoned by everyone, alone,

Like a bark abandoned at sea,
Prey to the savage wave.
. . . .
For a long time my solitary bark
Has scudded over the savage wave
. . . .
The night darkens, the storm rages,
My bark quickly rushes along.

In Marlinsky: "Like the debris of a shipwreck, I was cast up by the storm on the deserted shore of Nature" ("Farewell to the Caspian").

Как обломок кораблекрушения, выброшен был я бурею на пустынный берег Природы (Прощание с Каспием)

In Lermontov's poem "At the Mercy of a Marvelous Power" (1832) we find:

По произволу дивной власти
Я выкинут из царства страсти,
Как после бури на песок
Волной расшибенный челнок.

At the mercy of a marvelous power
I was cast out from the realm of passion,
Like a bark smashed by a wave,
[Found] on the beach after a storm.

Later this simile is used in "The Boyar Orsha":

Но узник был невозмутим,
Бесчувственно внимал он им.
Так бурей брошен на песок
Худой, увязнувший челнок,
Лишенный весел и гребцов,
Недвижим ждет напор валов.

But the prisoner was imperturbable,
Unfeelingly he listened to them .
Thus a leaky, bemired bark
Cast on the shore by a storm
Bereft of oars and oarsmen

55

Motionless awaits the force of the waves.

We encounter it in altered form in *Masquerade:*

> Опять мечты, опять любовь
> В пустой груди бушуют на просторе;
> Изломанный челнок, я снова брошен в море!
> Вернусь ли к пристани я вновь?
>
> (Действие 1-е, сц. III, выход 11)

> Again dreams, again love
> Rage on the expanse [of my] empty breast:
> A broken bark, I again was cast at sea!
> Will I return again to the harbor?
>
> (Act I, Scene III, Entrance II)

Another equally traditional image is that of a leaf driven by a storm or withering on a dry branch. It originates in French literature: Arnaud's poem "De la tige detachée," included in anthologies, became especially popular not only in French but also in Russian poetry. Arnaud's poem was translated by Zhukovsky, V. Pushkin (in the form of a fable), Davydov, and others; from this, as in the first case, began the comparison of human life to a leaf, which crops up in different poets of the 30s. Here is Zhukovsky's translation "A Leaf" (1818):

> От дружней ветки отлученный,
> Скажи, листок уединенный,
> Куда летишь?.. "Не знаю сам;
> Гроза разбила дуб родимый;
> С тех пор по долам, по горам
> По воле случая носимый,
> Стремлюсь, куда велит мне рок,
> Куда на свете все стремится,
> Куда и лист лавровый мчится,
> И легкий розовый листок."

> Parted from a friendly branch
> Tell me, little solitary leaf,
> Where are you flying?.. "I myself know not;
> The storm destroyed my native oak;
> Since then along vales, along mountains
> Borne by the will of chance

56

I rush wherever fate commands me,
Where *everything* in the world rushes,
Where even the laurel leaf races,
And the delicate little rose leaf."

We find a clear trace of the concluding lines of this poem in Kozlov:

Летучий вихрь равно в полях разносит
Ковыль-траву и розовый листок.

("Станцы")

In the fields the flying whirlwind scatters
The feather-grass and the little rose leaf.

("Stanzas")

He also employs a variation of this simile, the original of which belongs to Thomas Moore: "Thus the leaf withers on the severed branch" (translation of Moore's "Irish Melody"). Similar similes crop up in the most diverse poets of the time: in M. S. ("Atenei," 1830, part II): "torn from a branch by the storm, flies, whirls the tree-leaf... And I, a stranger in this land" etc.;[25] in A. Odoevsky: "And your life, like a leaf before the storm, will begin to tremble." In Lermontov we have:

Везде один, природы сын,
Не знал он друга меж людей:
Так бури ток сухой листок
Мчит жертвой посреди степей!...

("Портреты"   1829   г.)

Everywhere alone, a son of nature,
Among people he knew no friend:
Thus the storm's current whirls the dry leaflet along
A victim amidst the steppes.

("Portraits," 1829)

Так куст растет над бездною морскою,
И лист, грозой оборванный, плывет
По произволу странствующих вод.

("Дай руку мне" 1831 г.)

Thus a bush grows over the sea abyss
And a leaf, plucked by a storm, floats
At the mercy of the wandering waters.

("Give me your hand," 1831)

И полетел знакомою дорогой,
Как пыльный лист, оторванный грозой,
Летит крутясь по степи голубой!
("Аул Бастунджи" 1831 г.)

And he flew by a familiar path
Like a dusty leaf torn off by a storm
Flies twirling over the blue steppe!
("Aul Bastundzhi," 1831)

Он жил забыт и одинок -
Грозой оторванный листок.
("Демон" 1833 г.)

He lived forgotten and alone
A leaflet torn off by a storm.
("Demon," 1833)

Угрюм и одинок,
Грозой оторванный листок,
Я вырос в сумрачных стенах.
("Мцыри," 4)

Sullen and alone,
A leaf torn off by a storm,
I grew up within gloomy walls,
("The Novice," 4)

Finally, in 1841 Lermontov develops this traditional simile into an entire ballad, complicating Zhukovsky's simple allegory by means of a special plot-line:

Дубовый листок оторвался от ветки родимой
И в степь укатился, жестокою бурей гонимый,
и т.д.

The little oak leaf was torn from its native branch
And rolled away across the steppe, driven by a cruel storm,
etc.

In one instance Lermontov, as if tired of it, replaced this traditional simile with another. The last two lines of the poem "The Plague" (1830):

58

И душу рок от тела оторвал,
И будто сноп на землю он упал —

    And fate tore his soul from his body
    And he fell to the earth like a sheaf

have the following draft variant (autograph of the Lermontov Museum, notebook VIII, No. 16):

И оторвал от тела душу рок,
Как ветер от сухих ветвей листок.

    And fate tore [his] soul from [his] body,
    As the wind a little leaf from dry branches.

"Stanzas" of 1831 ("I gaze ahead through the gloom of years") concludes with the lines:

Ненужный член в пиру людском,
Младая ветвь на пне сухом; -
В ней соку нет, хоть зелена,-
Дочь смерти - смерть ей суждена! -

    An unnecessary member at the human feast,
    A young branch on a dry stump;
    Though green, there is no sap in it,
    A daughter of death - it is doomed to death!

In Zhukovsky's "The Prisoner of Chillon" we find (these lines are not in Byron):

Без места на пиру земном,
Я был бы лишний гость на нем.

    Without a place at the earthly feast,
    I would have been an unnecessary guest at it.

In Polezhaev ("The Living Corpse"):

И, член ненужный бытия,
Не оскверню собой природы.

And an unnecessary member of existence,
I will not defile nature with my presence.

Also in Polezhaev ("Man" - from Lamartine):

Несчастный, страждущий и смертными презренный,
Я буду жалкий член живого бытия.

Unfortunate, suffering and despised by mortals
I will be a pathetic member of living existence.

In A. Odoevsky ("Elegy," 1830):

Как званный гость или случайный,
Пришел он в этот чуждый мир.

Like an invited or chance guest
He came to this alien world.

An echo of this simile is in Lermontov's "Meditation" (1838):

И жизнь уж нас томит, как ровный путь без цели,
Как пир на празднике чужом.

And life torments us, like an aimless, even path,
Like a feast at another's celebration.

And in "The First of January" (1840):

И шум толпы людской спугнет мечту мою,
На праздник незванную гостью.

And the noise of the human crowd will frighten my dream,
Like a guest uninvited to the celebration.

Zhukovsky has a poem, "The Prisoner to a Moth" (from de Maistre, 1813), consisting of an extended monologue of the prisoner addressed to a moth which has flown into his dungeon. It concludes with the following stanza:

Падут железные затворы -

Детей, супругу, небеса,
Родимый край, холмы, леса
Опять мои увидят взоры...
Но что?... я цепью загремел;
Сокрылся призрак-обольститель;
Вспорхнул эфирный посетитель...
Постой!... но он уж улетел.

> The iron bars will fall -
> Again my eyes will see
> [My] children, wife, the heavens
> [My] beloved land, hills, forests...
> But what is this?... I rattled my chain;
> The captivating phantom disappeared;
> The ethereal visitor took wing...
> Stop!... but already it had flown away.

Kozlov has a poem, "To the Countess Pototskaya" ("I have not seen your eyes"), constructed on a like simile where we read:

И я знаком моей мечтой
С твоей пленительной красой,
И голос нежный знаю я -
Он слышен в сердце у меня.

Так узник в мрачной тишине
Мечтает о красах природы,
О солнце ярком, о луне,
О том, что видел в дни свободы;

Уснет ли он - в его очах
Леса, река, поля в цветах,
И пробудясь вздыхает он.
Благословляя светлый сон.

> And I am familiar in my dream
> With your enchanting beauty,
> And I know your tender voice -
> It can be heard in my heart...
>
> Thus the prisoner in gloomy quietude
> Dreams of the beauties of nature,
> About the bright sun, the moon,

About what he saw in days of freedom;

If he falls asleep there will be in his eyes
Forests, a river, fields in blossom,
And awakening he sighs.
Blessing the bright dream.

In Ryleev's "Voynarovsky" we read:

Так посещает в подземелье
Почти убитого тоской
Страдальца-узника порой
Души минутное веселье.

Thus from time to time in the dungeon
A momentary joy of soul
Visits the suffering prisoner
Almost crushed by grief.

On the other hand, Polezhaev has a poem "Claims" in which the old
literary allegory ("man-prisoner"), preserving its traditional character, is
realized. Here there is a monologue beyond which lies no secondary meaning:

Зачем игрой воображенья
Картины счастья рисовать,
Зачем душевные мученья
Тоской опасной растравлять?
. . . .
Уже рукой ожесточенной
Берусь за пагубную сталь,
Уже рассудок мой смущенный
Забыл и горе, и печаль!..
Готов!.. Но цепь порабощенья
Гремит на скованных руках
                    и т.д.

Why with the play of imagination
Draw pictures of happiness;
Why aggravate spiritual torments
With dangerous grief?
. . . .
Already with an embittered hand

I take up the fatal steel,
Already my troubled reason
Has forgotten both grief and sadness!...
I am ready!... But the chains of thralldom
Rattle on fettered hands

                        etc.

As was the case with the allegory "man-bark," thus in this instance, too, a bit remains from the whole ("man-prisoner"), which also is employed by Lermontov:

Как цепь гремит за узником, за мной
Так мысль о будущем, и нет иной.
                        ("Подражание Байрону" 1830 г.)

As the chain rattles behind the prisoner, behind me [rattles]
Thus the thought of the future, and there is no other.
                        ("Imitation of Byron," 1830)

В вечерний час дождливых облаков
Я наблюдал разорванный покров;
Лиловые, с багряными краями,
Одни еше грозят, и над скалами
Волшебный замок, чудо древних дней,
Растет в минуту; но еще скорей
Его рассеет ветра дуновенье!
Так прерывает резкий звук цепей
Преступного страдальца сновиденье,
Когда он зрит холмы своих полей...
                        ("Измаил-Бей" 1832 г., ч. 1-ая, 11)

At eventide I observed
The tattered cover of rain clouds;
Lilac with crimson edges
Some still threaten, and above the cliffs
An enchanted castle, a marvel of ancient days,
Grows in a moment; but still more quickly
A breath of wind scatters it!
Thus the harsh sound of chains interrupts
The dream of a criminal sufferer,
When he beholds the hills of his fields...
                        ("Izmail-Bei," 1832, Part I, II)

In the last instance the thematic artificiality of the simile--its weak motivation--is striking. It was at hand and Lermontov uses it not because precisely this one fits, rather because he needs a simile here for stylistic and compositional considerations, even if it is one such as this.

One simile in Byron's "The Prisoner of Chillon" was transferred to Zhukovsky's translation and is later encountered in Marlinsky ("The Raids"):

> I had no thought, no feeling - none,
> Among the stones I stood a stone.

In Zhukovsky:

> Без пямяти , без бытия,
> Меж камней хладным камнем я.

> Without memory, without existence,
> Among the stones I am a cold stone.

We have in Marlinsky (about the imprisoned Prince Serebryany) "and he, in a burst of impotent rage, shaking his chains and again struck by hopelessness, fell, like a cold stone among stones."

In Lermontov we find:

> На жизнь надеяться страшась,
> Живу как камень меж камней.
>
> ("Отрывок" 1830 г.)

> Fearing to hope for life
> I live like a stone among stones.
>
> ("Fragment" 1830)

In Polezhaev:[26]

> Я весь дрожал, я трепетал,
> Как злой преступник перед казнью.
>
> ("Кольцо")

> I was trembling all over, I shook
> Like an evil prisoner before execution.
>
> ("A Ring")

In Lermontov:

Гляжу на будущность с боязнью,
Гляжу на прошлое с тоской,
И, как преступник перед казнью,
Ищу кругом души родной.

(1837)

I look to the future with fear,
I look to the past with longing,
And like a prisoner before execution,
All around I seek a kindred soul.

(1837)

Such expressions as "a plaything of passions" or "a grave dweller," constant in Lermontov, are poetic cliches used by Polezhaev, Kozlov and Odoevsky.

Lermontov's poem "The day will come, and condemned by the world" (1830) concludes with lines which go back to Venevitinov's poem "Testament" or to a common source:

Но если , если над моим позором
    Смеяться станешь ты,
И возмутишь неправедным укором
    И речью клеветы
Обиженную тень, - не жди пощады;
    Как червь к душе твоей
Я прилеплюсь, и каждый миг отрады
    Несносен будет ей,
И будешь помнить прежнюю беспечность,
    Не зная воскресить,
И будет жизнь тебе долга, как вечность,
    А все не будешь жить.

But if, if you should begin
    to laugh at my disgrace
And with unjust reproach and slanderous
        speech enrage
[My] offended shadow - do not expect mercy;
    Like a worm, to your soul
I will fasten myself, and every instant of joy
    Will be unbearable to it,
And you will recall former carefreeness

                    Not knowing how to resurrect it,
                    And life will be as long as eternity for you,
                    And yet you will not live.

In Venevitinov:

            Сей дух, как вечно бдящий взор,
            Твой будет спутник неотступной,
            И если памятью преступной
            Ты изменишь... беда! с тех пор
            Я тайно облекусь в укор,
            К душе прилипну вероломной,
            В ней пищу мщения найду,
            И будет сердцу грустно, томно, -
            А я как червь не отпаду.

                    This spirit, like an eternally vigilant glance
                    Will be your inseparable companion
                    And if by criminal reminiscence
                    You will be unfaithful... Woe! From that time
                    I secretly will clothe myself in reproach
                    I will stick to your perfidious soul
                    I will find the food of vengeance in it,
                    And your heart will be sad, weary, -
                    And like a worm I will not fall away.

Verse formulae, to which Lermontov constantly was drawn, often prove to be borrowed. At the end of Kozlov's "Natalya Dolgorukaya" are the lines:

            Но сердце, но мечты, но струны,
            Они во мне, со мной, мои.

                    But the heart, but the dreams, but the strings
                    They are in me, with me, mine.

Lermontov employs this formula, first in "A Confession," later in the poem "K*_*" ("My friend, vain striving," 1832), and then in "The Boyar Orsha" and "The Novice":

            Кого любил? - Отец святой,
            Вот что умрет во мне, со мной!
            . . . .

Не встретят их глаза чужие,
Они умрут во мне, со мной!
. . . .
Мне их назвать? - Отец святой,
Вот что умрет во мне, со мной!
. . . .
Воспоминанья тех минут
Во мне, со мной пускай умрут.

     Whom did I love? - Holy Father,
     That is what will die in me, with me!
     . . . .
     Other eyes will not meet them,
     They will die in me, with me!
     . . . .
     How shall I name them? - Holy Father,
     That is what will die in me, with me!
     . . . .
     Memories of those moments
     Let them die in me, with me.

Another formula, running through an entire series of Lermontov's works ("The 15th of July, 1830," "Weep, weep, people of Israel," "The Last Son of Freedom," "The Angel of Death," "Aul Bastundzhi," "Izmail Bei") originates in Zhukovsky and Kozlov. We read in "The Prisoner of Chillon" (chapter IX):

В оцепенении стоял,
Без памяти, без бытия

. . . .
Но странный мир какой-то был,
Без неба, света и светил,
Без времени, без дней и лет,
Без промысла, без благ и бед
           и т.д.

     In a torpor he stood
     Without memory, without existence
     . . . .
     Some strange world existed then,
     Without sky, light and luminaries,
     Without time, without days and years,
     Without Providence, without good and misfortune
                               etc.

In Kozlov ("Natalya Dolgorukaya"):

Но есть пора: в томленьи бед
Ни сил, ни дум, ни чувства нет.

But there is a time: in the languor of misfortunes
There is neither strength, nor thought, nor feeling.

This syntactical system attracted Lermontov's attention by its emotional force, and we find: "Without friendship, without hopes, without strength," "Without thoughts, without feelings, amidst valleys," "Without thoughts, without trembling, without tears," "Almost without feelings, without thoughts, without strength," "Scarcely breathing, without tears, without thoughts, without words."

The very same chapter of "The Prisoner of Chillon," in Zhukovsky concludes with the words:

Задавленный тяжелой мглой,
Недвижный, темный и немой.

Crushed by heavy gloom
Immobile, dark and mute.

In Lermontov we find ("Epitaph," 1830):

Стоял, очей не обтирая,
Недвижный, хладный и немой.[27]

He stood, not wiping his eyes,
Immobile, cold and mute.

If one were to pay special attention to them, of course, the number of such comparisons could be greatly increased. What is important for me here is only to confirm by examples the general proposition that Lermontov does not create new materials but operates with ready-made material. Russian criticism considers this kind of artistic method reprehensible; therefore, probably until now comparisons between Lermontov and Byron have made reference to very few concrete, textual citations: they compromise the traditional view of poetry as the expression of an individual "perception of the world" or the direct emanation of the poet's soul. In point of fact, artistic creativity is *work*; the artistic piece, as the product of this work, is a *thing*.

The use of ready-made material is just as lawful, natural and imperative in this work as in any other. For the purpose of weighting lyric poetry with thought, for the creation of "memorable verse lines," Lermontov needed to have at hand a large stock of emotional formulae, similes, and the like. He draws this material from ready-made, literary stocks, in the process remaining if not an "original," then in any case an independent poet. And this is because his artistic *method*--that very "ability to fuse the most heterogeneous verse lines into a harmonious whole," about which Kyukhelbeker wrote, is independent and historically actual. The fundamental principle of this method is the transformation of lyric poetry into a pathetic confession, the sharpening and intensifying of the personal element, the creation of a special "I" which looks at the entire world from the point of view of its own fate and makes this fate a world problem:

> Я рожден, чтоб целый мир был зритель
> Торжества иль гибели моей.

> I was born so that the entire world would be a spectator
> Of my triumph or ruin.

This was the last tremor of Russian classical lyric poetry, just as the last tremor of the lyric poetry of the Symbolists was Blok's intense "I."

4

In the creative work of the type of artist who is "emotional" (not by nature but by method), who is concerned not so much about the harmoniousness and originality of construction as about its expressiveness, not only the widespread use of ready-made material can be observed, but also the systematic repetition of one's own earlier prepared segments; this lends a somewhat monotonous character to their style. Such a seeming contradiction (after all, genuine spiritual emotion must be expressed in a new form each time because it is experienced anew) becomes clear if one acknowledges artistic creation as work, and "emotionalism" as a specific stylistic method. The development of this method naturally leads away from tasks of construction, from the working out of plot details and new material; attention is concentrated upon the use and the arrangement of expressive formulae, "memorable lines," formed once and for all. Such is the character of the self-repetitions with which Lermontov's text abounds. Already in 1848 V. Plaksin took note of this peculiarity and, comparing "The Novice" with "The Boyar Orsha," wrote: "It is difficult to understand and still more difficult to explain why the poet compels his protagonists to repeat such lengthy tirades, which have been expressed in other passages by other figures....The genius, in accord with the characteristics of his creative nature, creates not in parts, individually and in chance sequence, but rather a whole, with the full number and volume of parts necessary for harmonious creation; that is why the genius never repeats what he creates. But when passion guides the movement of poetic forces, then an incompleteness and incoherence of creation and a repetition of images and scenes is an inevitable consequence" (*Severnoe obozrenie*, 1848, No. 3).

Of course, one can find recurrent elements of one kind or another in every writer (most often in the realm of plot); but, in the first place, their number usually is very limited and, above all, they are not transferred from one work to another, but only coincide in certain common features. Moreover, these similarities usually are found in mature pieces, when a system of artistic devices (method) is already acquiring a wholly stable character; the youthful initial work remains to the side. There is something completely different in Lermontov. His repetitions are literal transfers of separate segments, as cliches formed once and for all, so that sometimes a new poem to a significant degree proves to be a summary in relation to what has gone before. We have a most striking example of such treatment of material in the narrative poems "A Confession" (1830), "The Boyar Orsha" (1836), and "The Novice" (1840), but I shall speak of them later. Coupled with Lermontov's propensity for elaborating "memorable verse lines" (*pointes*), which we noted above, recurrent cliches of this type can serve not only as material for simple comparisons, but for study and analysis as well. As one might expect, what recurs primarily in Lermontov are all kinds of lyrical formulae, which often are linked with similes. For the most part they serve as tag lines for individual chapters, lines, or entire works, gaining in semantic force here. Their transference from one work to another, of course, results from the fact that the work written earlier has, on the whole, come to be considered unsuccessful; therefore, that portion is taken from it which is worthy of attention and capable of producing the appropriate impression in another context.

The 1830 poem "It is time for the heart to be at rest," about which I have spoken above, concludes with a condensed lyrical formula, followed by a simile:

> Но от сердечного недуга
> Не могла ты утаить;
> Слишком знаем мы друг друга,

Чтоб друг друга позабыть.
Так расселись под громами,
Видел я, в единый миг
Пощаженные веками
Два утеса бреговых;

и т.д. (см. выше)

But you could not conceal
The ailment of the heart;
We know each other too well
To forget one another.
Thus in a single instant
I saw two shoreline cliffs
Spared by the ages,
Parted by lightning.

etc. (See above.)

As is apparent in the manuscript, the poem did not satisfy Lermontov; its middle section (verses 9 - 16) has been crossed out; but its concluding formula was used in another poem of that year: "К*₋*" ("I will not humble myself before you"). Here this formula looks sudden and poorly motivated because the entire tone of the poem is completely different:

Я горд! - прости - люби другого,
Мечтай любовь найти в другом: -
Чего б то ни было земного
Я не соделаюсь рабом.
К чужим горам, под небо юга
Я удалюся, может быть;
Но слишком знаем мы друг друга,
Чтобы друг друга позабыть.
Отныне стану наслаждаться
И в страсти стану клясться всем;
Со всеми буду я смеяться,
А плакать не хочу ни с кем

и т.д.

I am proud! - Farewell - love another,
Dream of finding love in another:
Whatever there is earthly [in me]
I will not make myself a slave of.
To alien mountains, under a southern sky

Perhaps I shall withdraw;
But we know each other too well
To forget one another.
Henceforth I shall take pleasure
And in passion swear to all:
I shall laugh with everyone,
For I do not wish to cry with anyone.

                                    etc.

A link with Byron's "Stanzas" ("One struggle more"), translated by Kozlov ("To the Tirza"), can be seen in the last lines:

Хочу пиров, хочу похмелья,
Бездушным в свете стану жить,
Со всеми рад делить веселья,
Ни с кем же горя не делить.

I want feasts, I want intoxication,
I shall live soullessly in the world,
I am happy to share joy with everyone,
Sharing grief with none.

Regarding the simile (taken from the epigraph supplied by Byron), as I said
earlier it was transferred to another poem ("Romance," 1830).

In the poem "Night"(1830) ("I am alone in the stillness of the night")
there are two memorable passages which especially stand out, in the middle
and at the end:

Как мог я не любить тот взор?
Презренья женского кинжал
Меня пронзил,.... - но нет - с тех пор
Я все любил, - я все страдал -
. . . .
Желал я на другой предмет
Излить огонь страстей своих. -
Но память, слезы первых лет!
Кто устоит противу их? -

How could I not love that gaze?
The dagger of feminine contempt
Pierced me... but no, since that time
I have continued to love, -- I have continued to suffer, --
. . . .
I wished upon another object

72

To pour the fire of my passions.
But memory, the tears of first years!
Who will withstand them?

Like the majority of Lermontov's youthful verses it is very drawn out and not concise with respect to composition. Lermontov takes these two passages and inserts them into the narrative poem "The Last Son of Freedom":

И Вадим
Любил.- Но был ли он любим?........
Нет! - равнодушной Леды взор
Презренья холод оковал:
Отвергнут витязь; но с тех пор
Он все любил, он все страдал.
До униженья, до мольбы
Он не хотел себя склонить;
Мог презирать удар судьбы
И мог об нем не говорить.
Желал он на другой предмет
Излить огонь страстей своих;
Но память, слезы многих лет!..
Кто устоит противу них? --

And Vadim
Loved. But was he loved?...
No! The cold of contempt
Fettered Leda's indifferent gaze.
The hero was rejected; but since then
He continued to love, he continued to suffer.
To humiliation, to entreaty
He did not wish to bend himself
He could despise the blow of fate
And did not have to speak about it.
He wished upon another object
To pour the fire of his passions;
But memory, the tears of many years!...
Who will withstand them?

The draft of a lyric was ultimately used in the narrative poem in this way. In Lermontov one and the same formula can appear now in a narrative poem, now in a lyric, constituting a kind of saying. In the narrative poem "Dzhyulio" (1830) the description of a meeting with Melina concludes with the lines:

я не смел дохнуть,
Покуда взор, весь слитый из огня,
На землю томно не упал с меня -
Ах! он стрелой во глубь мою проник! -
- Не выразил бы чувств моих в сей миг
Ни ангельский, ни демонский язык!....

> I did not dare to breathe
> Until that gaze, all smelted of fire,
> Languidly fell from me to the earth.
> Ah! It pierced my depths like an arrow!
> --At that instant neither angelic nor demonic tongue
> Could have expressed my feelings!....

We find the last formula in the poem "The 11th day of June 1831," after the stanza about the "twilight of the soul," which also has its own history. We read at the end of "Dzhyulio":

Есть сумерки души во цвете лет,
Меж радостью и горем полусвет;
Жмет сердце безотчетная тоска;
Жизнь ненавистна, но и смерть тяжка.[28]

> There is a twilight of the soul in the flower of life
> A half-light between joy and grief;
> An unaccountable sorrow wrings the heart;
> Life is hateful, but death too is burdensome.

In somewhat altered form this formula is transferred to "The Lithuanian Woman"(1830):

Есть сумерки души, несчастья след,
Когда ни мрака в ней, ни света нет;
Она сама собою стеснена,
Жизнь ненавистна ей, и смерть страшна;
И небо обвинить нельзя ни в чем,
И как на зло, все весело кругом!

> There is a twilight of the soul, a trace of misfortune,
> When there is neither darkness nor light in it;
> It is oppressed by itself,
> Life is hateful to it, and death is fearful;
> And it is impossible to charge heaven with anything,

And, as if out of malice, everything around is gay!

These two formulae were joined in the poem "The 11th day of June, 1831," indicating that by that time both the narrative poems of "Dzyulio" and "The Lithuanian Woman" already were regarded by Lermontov as a stock of material which could be used in other pieces:

Есть время - леденеет быстрый ум;
Есть сумерки души, когда предмет
Желаний мрачен; усыпленье дум;
Меж радостью и горем полусвет;
Душа сама собою стеснена,
Жизнь ненавистна, но и смерть страшна,
Находишь корень мук в себе самом,
И небо обвинить нельзя ни в чем.

Я к состоянью этому привык,
Но ясно выразить его б не мог
Ни ангельский, ни демонский язык:
Они таких не ведают тревог.

There comes a time when the quick mind congeals;
There are twilights of the soul, when the object
Of desires is sombre; the lulling of thoughts;
A half-light between joy and grief;
The soul is constrained of itself,
Life is hateful, but death too is fearful,
One finds the root of torment in oneself,
And it is impossible to charge heaven with anything.

I am accustomed to this condition,
But neither an angelic nor demonic tongue
Could express it clearly:
They do not know such anxieties.

In "Izmail-Bei" (1832) we again find:

Не мог бы описать подобный миг
Ни ангельский, ни демонский язык.

Neither an angelic nor demonic tongue
Could describe a like instant.

Another simile has a long history; from the dedication to *"The Span-iards"* (1829-30) and from "The Lithuanian Woman" (1830) it is transferred to this very same poem "1831," and from there to "The Boyar Orsha" (1836). The dedication to *"The Spaniards"* concludes with the lines:

Но ты меня понять могла;
Страдальца ты не осмеяла,
Ты с беспокойного чела
Морщины ранние сгоняла:

Так над гробницею стоит
Береза юная, склоняя
С участием ветки на гранит,
Когда ревет гроза ночная! -

But you could understand me;
You did not mock a sufferer,
You drove early furrows
From a troubled brow:

Thus a young birch stands
Over a sepulchre, sympathetically
Bending its branches to the granite
When the night storm rages!

"The Lithuanian Woman" ends with a tale of how Arseny's wife prays for him in a monastery. This tale concludes with a maxim (*sentenciia*), to which is joined the simile of the birch tree, which no longer is growing over a tomb but in the crevice of a ruin:

В печальном только сердце может страсть
Иметь неограниченную власть.
Так в трещине развалин иногда
Береза вырастает: молода
И зелена, и взоры веселит,
И украшает сумрачный гранит;
И часто отдыхающий пришлец
Грустит о ней и мыслит; наконец,
Порывам бурь и зною предана,
Увянет преждевременно она!
Но что ж? - Усилья вихря и дождей

76

Не могут обнажить ее корней,
И пыльный лист, встречая жар дневной,
Трепещет все на ветке молодой.

Only in a sad heart can passion
Possess limitless power.
Thus sometimes in the crevice of a ruin
A birch grows: young
And green, it gladdens the gaze
And adorns the sombre granite;
And often the resting stranger
Grieves for it and reflects; finally,
Abandoned to the heat and gusts of storms
It will wither prematurely!
But what of this? --The efforts of the whirlwind
                                    and the rains
Can not bare its roots,
And greeting the heat of the day, a dusty leaf
Yet flutters on the young branch.

In such form this simile is transferred to the poem "1831" with this difference: the maxim is placed not at the beginning, but at the end. Later this maxim is separated from the simile: the simile will occur in "The Boyar Orsha," and the maxim turns up in the tale "Vadim," where it concludes the XIV chapter: "Vadim possessed an unhappy soul over which a single thought sometimes could acquire limitless power." In "The Boyar Orsha" the birch simile completes the description of the sullen Orsha and his daughter, joining both versions of the simile: a birch standing over a tomb and a birch in the crevice of a ruin:

В его глазах она росла
Свежа, невинна, весела,
Цветок грядущего святой,
Былого памятник живой!
Так средь развалин иногда
Растет береза: молода,
Мила над плитами гробов
Игрою шепчущих листов,
И та холодная стена
Ее красой оживлена!.....

She grew in his eyes
Fresh, innocent, gay,

A sacred flower of the future,
A living monument of the past!
Thus sometimes amidst a ruin
A birch grows: young,
Pleasing above the gravestones
With the play of whispering leaves
And that cold wall
Is enlivened by its beauty!...

The link between the poem "1831" and the narrative poems of 1830 ("Dzhyulio" and "The Lithuanian Woman") is especially interesting for yet another reason. The iambic pentameter with masculine rhymes taken by Lermontov from English poetry, and which he uses particularly often in 1830 and employs in the narrative poems in place of the iambic tetrameter traditional for Russian narrative poems, ceases to appeal to him. The narrative poems of 1831 are written either in iambic tetrameter (solely with masculine rhymes as in "Azrail," or with alternating masculine and feminine rhymes as in "The Angel of Death" and "Kally"), or in iambic pentameter but with alternating masculine and feminine rhymes, and, moreover, in octaves ("Aul Bastundzhi"). In this year he attempts to write "The Demon" in the verse line of "The Lithuanian Woman" ("It [?] flew across the blue sky"), but drops it at the very beginning. Disappointed in the suitability of this line for the narrative poem, in 1831 Lermontov attempts to use it in writing a special type of meditation, filled with aphorisms and formulae like "The 11th day of June, 1831" or "I saw the shadow of bliss." Later he abandons even these attempts. Apparently Lermontov's disappointmet with this verse line was a consequence of the fact that the works so written acquired an excessively prosaic inflection owing to the masculine rhymes and forceful *enjambements*.

Thus, material from "Dzhyulio" and "The Lithuanian Woman" is scattered into different works: "The 11th day of June, 1831," "The Boyar Orsha," "Izmail-Bei," "Vadim." All of this material is either condensed lyrical formulae-sayings or similes.

Here are some examples:

Безумцы! не могли понять,
Что легче плакать, чем страдать
Без всяких признаков страданья.
                    (Конец "Эпитафии" 1830 г.)

И ангел знал - и как не знать? -
Что безнадежности печать

В спокойном холоде молчанья,
Что легче плакать, чем страдать
Без всяких признаков страданья!
("Ангел Смерти" 1831 г.)

Fools! They could not understand
That it is easier to cry than to suffer
Without any signs of suffering.
(The end of "Epitaph," 1830)

And the angel knew- how could he not know?
That the stamp of hopelessness
Is in the calm coldness of silence,
That it is easier to cry than to suffer
Without any signs of suffering!
("The Angel of Death," 1831)

Отец их был убит в чужом краю,
А мать Селим убил своим рожденьем,
И хоть невинный, начал жизнь свою,
Как многие кончают - преступленьем.
("Аул Бастунджи," 1831 г.)

Как лишний меж людьми, своим рожденьем
Он душу не обрадовал ничью,
И хоть невинный, начал жизнь свою,
Как многие кончают -- преступленьем.
("Измаил-Бей," 1832 г.)

Their father was killed in an alien land
And Selim killed his mother in birth
And, though innocent, he began his life
As many finish theirs - with a crime.
("Aul Bastundzhi," 1831)

Superfluous among people, with his birth
He had not gladdened any soul,
And though innocent, he began his life
As many finish theirs - with a crime.
("Izmail-Bei," 1832)

Он стал на свете сирота.
Душа его была пуста.
Он сел на камень гробовой,

И по челу провел рукой;
Но грусть - ужасный властелин:
С чела не сгладил он морщин!
            ("Посл. сын вольности" 1830 г.)

Казалось, вспомнить он старался
Рассказ ужасный, и желал
Себя уверить он, что спал;
Желал бы счесть он все мечтою...
И по челу провел рукою;
Но грусть - жестокий властелин!
С чела не сгладил он морщин
            ("Измаил-Бей" 1832 г.)

He became an orphan in the world,
His soul was empty.
He sat on a gravestone,
And ran his hand across his brow;
But sadness is a terrible master:
He did not smooth the furrows from his brow!
            (The Last Son of Freedom," 1830)

It seemed he was trying to recall
The horrible tale, and wished
To assure himself that he had been sleeping;
He would have wished to consider everything a dream...
And he ran his hand across his brow;
But sadness is a cruel master!
He did not smooth the furrows from his brow.
            ("Izmail-Bei," 1832)

Когда-нибудь - и скоро - я
Оставлю ношу бытия...
Скажи, ужель одна могила
Ничтожный в мире будет след
Того, чье сердце столько лет
Мысль о ничтожестве томила?
            ("Ангел Смерти" 1831 г.)

Ужель степная лишь могила
Ничтожный в мире будет след
Того, чье сердце столько лет
Мысль о ничтожестве томила?

("Измаил-Бей" 1832 г.)

Sometime - and soon - I
Will abandon the burden of existence...
Tell me, is it possible that only a grave
Will be the insignificant trace in the world
Of him whose heart for so many years
The thought of insignificance tormented?
("The Angel of Death," 1831)

Is it possible that only a steppe grave
Will be the insignificant trace in the world
Of him whose heart for so many years
The thought of insignificance tormented?
("Izmail-Bei," 1832)

It is apparent from these examples that the narrative poem "Izmail-Bei" incorporates material from preceding poems: from "The Last Son of Freedom," "The Angel of Death" and "Aul Bastundzhi." In turn, something from "Izmail-Bei" is transferred to the next narrative poem "Khadzhi-Abrek" (1834).

The 1830 poem "K*.*" ("When your friend with prophetic grief") may serve as an interesting example of how Lermontov uses his old material. Its first part was used later in the poem "Do not laugh at my prophetic grief" (1837), and the second part ("He was born for peaceful inspirations") first became part of the 1832 poem ("He was born for happiness, for hope and peaceful inspirations," etc.), and later, part of the poem "To the Memory of A. I. Odoevsky" (stanza II: "He was born for them, for the hopes of poetry and happiness," etc.). The second half of the poem "He was born for happiness" (1832) has its own history; it is transferred from here to the end of the poem "I look to the future with fear" (1837), and then into "Meditation" (1838).

In its significant portion the poem "To the Memory of A. I. Odoevsky" goes back to the narrative poem "Sashka." The third, fourth, and first part of the fifth stanzas of "To the Memory of A. I. Odoevsky" read like this:

Но он погиб далеко от друзей...
Мир сердцу твоему, мой милый Саша!
Покрытое землей чужих полей,
Пусть тихо спит оно, как дружба наша
В немом кладбище памяти моей.
Ты умер, как и многие, - без шума,

Но с твердостью. Таинственная дума
Еще блуждала на челе твоем,
Когда глаза закрылись вечным сном;
И то, что ты сказал перед кончиной,
Из слушавших тебя не понял ни единый...

И было ль то привет стране родной,
Названье ли оставленного друга?
Или тоска по жизни молодой,
Иль просто крик последнего недуга,
Кто скажет нам! твоих последних слов
Глубокое и горькое значенье...
Потеряно... Дела твои, и мненья,
И думы, все исчезло без следов,
Как легкий пар вечерних облаков:
Едва блеснут, их ветер вновь уносит...
Куда они, зачем, - откуда? - кто их спросит...

И после их на небе нет следа,
Как от любви ребенка безнадежной,
Как от мечты, которой никогда
Он не вверял заботам дружбы нежной!....

But he perished far from friends...
Peace to your heart, my dear Sasha!
Covered by the earth of foreign fields,
Let it sleep quietly, like our friendship,
In the mute graveyard of my memory.
You died, like many others, quietly
Yet steadfastly. An enigmatic thought
Still wandered on your brow,
When your eyes closed in eternal sleep;
And that which you said before the end
Not one who heard you understood...

And was it a greeting to [your] native land
Or the name of an abandoned friend?
Or grief for [your] young life
Or simply the shout of a final illness,
Who will tell us! Of your last words...
The deep and bitter meaning
Has been lost... Your affairs and opinions
And thoughts, all has disappeared without a trace,

Like the light vapor of evening clouds:
Scarcely they flash, [and] the wind bears them anew...
Whither are they, why, whence - who will ask them...

And afterwards there is no trace of them in the sky,
As of the hopeless love of a child,
As of the dream, which never
He entrusted to the cares of tender friendship!...

The first of the stanzas cited and the beginning of the second correspond to the III-IV stanzas of "Sashka," and the remainder is taken from stanzas CXXXVI-CXXXVII.

Apparently the origin of the last two stanzas, as well as the line "He was born for peaceful inspirations," which first appeared in 1830, is connected with A. Odoevsky's "Elegy" (1830), where we read:

Что вы печальны, дети снов?
Летучей жизни привиденья?
Как хороводы облаков,
С небес, по воле дуновенья,
Летят и тают в вышине,
Следов нигде не оставляя, -
Равно в подоблачной стране
Неслись вы! . . . .
. . . .
Кто был рожден для вдохновений
И мир в себе очаровал

и т.д.

Why are you sad, children of dreams?
Visions of a transient life
Like the clouds' round-dance
At the will of a breeze from the heavens
They fly and melt on high
Nowhere leaving a trace.
In like manner you rushed
Over the land beneath the clouds.
. . . .
Who was born for inspirations
And charmed the world in his person
etc.

It is interesting that in transferring stanza III from "Sashka" to "To the

Memory of A. I. Odoevsky," Lermontov preserved its structure (the rhyme scheme ababa/ccddee) intact, although the remaining stanzas of "To the Memory" have a different structure (ababcddccee - except the last one, where there are not 11, but 10 lines following the system ababcddcee). This proves that the stanzas cited were first in "Sashka."[29]

Thus, the poem "To the Memory of A. I. Odoevsky" turns out to be a complex fusion of material, which takes its origin back in 1830: a typical example of Lermontov's artistic work.

Separate links can be found between "Sashka" and "The Novice," between "The Boyar Orsha" and "The Demon," between "Sashka" and "A Fairy Tale for Children," between "Sashka" and "The First of January" (1840).

We read in "Sashka" (stanza LXXII):

> но без власти
> Венец казался бременем, и страсти,
> Впервые пробудясь, живым огнем
> Прожгли алтарь свой...
>
> и т.д.

> but without power
> The crown seemed a burden, and passions
> Once aroused, consumed their altar
> With a living fire....
>
> etc.

In "The Novice" we find:

> Я знал одной лишь думы власть, -
> Одну, но пламенную страсть:
> Она как червь во мне жила,
> Изгрызла душу и сожгла.
> . . . .
> Знай, этот пламень с юных дней
> Таяся жил в груди моей;
> Но ныне пищи нет ему,
> И он прожег свою тюрьму
>
> и т.д.

> I knew the power of but one thought, -
> A single, but fiery passion:

84

It lived in me like a worm
[It] gnawed through and consumed [my] soul.
. . . .
Know, this flame since youthful days
Secretly lived in my breast;
But nowadays it has no food
And it has consumed its prison.

etc.

Here one can see Lermontov's characteristic contamination of images, which destroys the unity of a simile or a metaphor (catachresis) and proves a lack of interest in the object of comparison: passion like a *worm* gnawed and *consumed* my soul. As we see, the word "consumed" is a remnant from another text ("the passions consumed their altar with a *living fire'*). I spoke earlier about the expression "an unnecessary member of the human feast": this also is a contamination of two texts: "a superfluous *guest* at the earthly *feast*" (Zhukovsky) and "an unnecessary *member* of *existence*" (Polezhaev).

Such examples confirm the dulling of semantic nuances in Lermontov's verse language.

Moreover, in the first four lines we have echoes of Podolinsky and Kozlov. In Podolinsky's narrative poem "The Beggar," which is very close to "The Novice" in type of verse line and style, [30] we read:

Но понял я, какую власть
Взяла над сердцем эта страсть,
И с этой страстью, видит бог,
Хотел бороться и не мог!

. . . .
Кто знает пламенную страсть,
Кто над собой изведал власть

и т.д.

But I understood what power
This passion had taken over my heart,
And with this passion, God sees,
I wished but could not struggle!

. . . .
Who knows a fiery passion,
Who has experienced this power over oneself

etc.

In Kozlov's "The Bride of Abydos" we read:

Она как червь - жилец могилы - [31]
Не утихает, не уснет;
И этот червь в душе гнездится,
Не терпит света, тьмы страшится.

> She, like a worm -- a grave dweller --
> Never ceases, will not sleep;
> And this worm nests in my soul,
> Endures not light, is fearful of the dark.

In "Sashka" an old house is described on whose walls can be seen the inscriptions:

Кто писал? С какою целью?
Грустил ли он иль предан был веселью?
Как надписи надгробные, оне
Рисуются узором по стене -
Следы давно погибших чувств и мнений,
Эпиграфы неведомых творений.

> Who was writing? For what purpose?
> Was he sad or devoted to merriment?
> Like the inscriptions on tombstones, they
> Are drawn in a pattern upon the wall -
> Traces of feelings and opinions long dead
> Epigraphs of unknown creations!...

The last formula is used at the end of a "A Fairy Tale for Children" (1839) in the description of a ball:

Улыбки, лица лгали так искуссно,
Что даже мне чуть-чуть не стало грустно;
Прислушаться хотел я - но едва
Ловил мой слух летучие слова,
Отрывки безымянных чувств и мнений -
Эпиграфы неведомых творений!...

> Smiles, faces lied so skilfully
> That even I almost became sad;
> I wished to listen - but my ear
> Scarcely caught the passing words,
> Fragments of nameless feelings and opinions,
> Epigraphs of unknown creations!...

The line about "epigraphs" looks strange in the new context: it is no longer a matter of inscriptions, but of fragments of conversations; but what is important for Lermontov is the use of the formula, and he takes it ready - made.

In "The Boyar Orsha" the description of the sullen old man's death ends with the lines:

Две яркие слезы текли
Из побелевших мутных глаз,
Собой лишь светлы, как алмаз.
Спокойны были все черты,
Исполнены той красоты,
Лишенной чувства и ума,
Таинственной, как смерть сама.

> Two bright tears flowed
> From lacklustre white eyes
> Themselves as bright as diamonds.
> All [his] features were tranquil
> Filled with that beauty,
> Devoid of feeling and intellect,
> Mysterious as death itself.

These lines were not suitable in "The Noivce," but later they were used in "The Demon," and precisely in the last sketch in the description of Tamara lying in the grave:

И ничего в ее лице
Не намекало о конце
В пылу страстей и упоенья;
И были все ее черты
Исполнены той красоты,
Как мрамор, чуждой выраженья,
Лишенной чувства и ума,
Таинственной, как смерть сама.

> And nothing in her face
> Hinted of the end
> In the heat of passions and ecstacy;
> And all her features were
> Filled with that beauty,
> Devoid of expression, like marble,
> Devoid of feeling and intellect
> Mysterious as death itself.

It turns out that one and the same formula serves as the conclusion both for the description of the death of the sullen old man Orsha and the description of the lovely princess Tamara lying in the grave. This example illustrates especially vividly the mosaic quality of Lermontov's work, the lack of "organic unity," of an interrelationship between this type of formulae and the thematic material. Along with the dulling of semantic nuances and the contamination of images linked to it, we see the disintegration of form and genre; a rupture between plot and stylistic material. Thus, the very same speech is pronounced by Arseny, the Spanish monk condemned by the Inquisition in "The Boyar Orsha," and the novice dying of his yearning for freedom.

We have traced Lermontov's main repetitions. As we see, they really are purely stylistic cliches which are not connected with the material of any one specific work, and that is why they roam through various works. While rejecting old works and inventing new situations and themes, Lermontov carefully preserves these elements, transferring them from one work to another and combining them. From this point of view the entire history of Lermontov's poetic creativity represents a persistent and intense reworking of what he had prepared during the years of early youth. Work on "The Demon," which runs throughout his entire creative life (1829-1841), proves to be neither a solitary nor exceptional instance. His main work is directed toward fusion, toward the motivated combining of prepared material: lyric formulae, similes, rhetorical maxims, etc. Hence the vagueness and indefiniteness of his genres. His lyric poetry inevitably assumes the character of extended meditations with fleeting, pathetic formulae, or it loses its keenness, and recalls Zhukovsky's, Kozlov's , Podolinsky's, etc., outlived "songs" or "romances." The narrative poem is transformed into a lyrical confession where the narrative and especially the descriptive part plays a secondary role, the role of conventional decoration which always may be altered. The more magnificent this decoration ("The Novice," "The Demon"), the stronger the impression of operatic sham. The sham is unable to create any illusion whatever, because the artists themselves, no matter how colorfully they are decked out in national dress, behave like genuine opera singers: they perform their arias as individual, independent numbers. In Lermontov's mature verse we must see an intense search for genres; one can predict that he will switch from intimate lyrical pieces to the development of an oratorical, declamatory style within the bounds of which his "memorable verse lines" will find a place. And on the ruins of the narrative poem ballads will arise in which remnants of the exotic decoration will find a haven.

CHAPTER II: VERSE OF THE SECOND PERIOD (1836-1841)

1

During his second period of creative activity (1836-1841) Lermontov wrote in all about 80 lyric poems. However, in terms of verse the years 1838-39 were very meagre; at this time Lermontov is occupied with prose. In the interval between his youthful verse and the verse of the new period Lermontov attempts to write dramas: *The Masquerade* and *Two Brothers* *(The Spaniards, Menschen und Leidenschaften,* and *A Strange Man* belong to the early period 1830-3l). If Lermontov employs chiefly English and French material in lyric poetry and the narrative poem, then here most noticeable of all are traces of his acquaintance with German drama: with Schiller *(Die Räuber, Kabale und Liebe),* with the theater of *Sturm und Drang,* and finally with the melodrama of Kotzebue.

The youthful pieces have a wholly melodramatic character. The *Sturm und Drang* style is curiously interwoven with scenes of daily life here, as in Schiller's *Kabale und Liebe,* where the elderly father's speech is written in comic everyday tones, and Ferdinand's speech is stylized in the spirit of Klinger's, Leisewitz's, and others' heroes. In Lermontov's scenes of daily life the tradition of 18th-century Russian comedy is revealed with its exaggerated coarseness of language. In *Menschen und Leidenschaften,* for example, Darya and Marfa Ivanovna speak in such language:

> "Marfa Iv.: Dashka, how did you dare give away two chickens today to the kitchen, and without asking me? Answer [me]!
> Darya: I'm guilty... I knew, Matushka, that two were a lot, but I had no time to report to your worship...
> Marfa Iv.: Fool! Swine! How are two a lot? Now we won't have anything to eat. Very likely you'll starve me to death from hunger! Do you know, right now and in my presence, I'll order them to slap you in the face...
> Darya (bowing): As you like, Madam! As you wish... We are your slaves..." etc.

Yury Volin's style is completely different:

> "Without you I would have no friend on whose breast I could pour out all my feelings, thoughts, hopes, dreams and doubts... I do not know... some strange presentiment has tormented me from the cradle. Often in the dark of night I have wept over cold pillows when I recalled that I had absolutely

no one, no one in the entire world besides you, but you were far away. In-
justices, spite--everything rained down on my head. It was as if a stormcloud,
having swept in, had fallen upon me and burst, and I stood like a stone--in-
sensible. From some mechanical impulse I stretched out my hand and heard
derisive laughter, but no one took my hand and it fell back upon my heart.
Heaven!...what does she wish to do? Tell me: yes! (Silence.) Why do you
not wish to say: yes! This word, this sound could restore my life, revive me
for happiness!....You do not wish to? What have I done to you--why are you
taking revenge on me so perfidiously? Is it possible a woman cannot love; is
it possible she is not joyful when she sees a man indebted to her for his bliss,
when she knows that it costs but one word, even if it should not come from
the heart..I am loved...loved...loved...now let all the ills of earth beset me--I
am contemptuous of you: she loves me...*she* is a creature such as Heaven
would be proud of...and she belongs to me! How rich I am!... May she choke
on that wretched estate!....O...now everything is clear....People, people...
people!....Why can I not love all of you as before?....I recognized you, hatred, the thirst for revenge...vengeance....Ha! ha! ha! How sweet it is, what
earthly nectar!..."

The difference in style is expressed not only in lexicon (in the choice of
words), but in the very construction of the phrases, in the syntax, the intonations. Yury's speech bears a pathetic character: exclamations alternate
with questions, phrases break off in ellipses, etc. It sounds wholly bookish,
larded like Lermontov's poetry with emphatic formulae, similes. This is intensified especially in the monologues, by means of which the denouement
usually is prepared. Before taking poison Yury utters a long monologue
which is extremely typical of German melodrama:

And he, my father, cursed me! And so terribly....At that moment when I
had sacrificed everything for him: the miserable old woman who would not
have endured this, my gratitude...At that very moment....Ha! ha! ha! O,
people, people!....Two, three words, the stupidest slander caused me to stand
here at the edge of the grave....Magnificent eternity! Magnificent memories!....O, if I could destroy myself! But no!....Yes! No! My soul has perished. I stand before my Creator. My heart does not tremble.... I prayed....
there was no salvation....I suffered....Nothing could touch it! (Sprinkles pow-
der in a glass.) O! I shall die....Truly, they will rejoice more at my death than
at my birth."[32]

The drama *A Strange Man* is written in this same style: it partially incorporates the preceding drama as also was done in the narrative poems.
Vladimir Arbenin's tirades correspond to Yury Volin's pathetic speeches.
The scene with Yury and the servant Ivan (Act 5, scene VIII: "Are you
well, barin?" etc.) is transferred here to Vladimir and Ivan (Scene XI). The
poem "The Beggar" (1830), in which a request for love is compared to a

request for a piece of bread, is rephrased here (a scene analogous to the one cited above):

> "Woman... Are you hesitating? Listen: if a dog emaciated from hunger would come crawling to your feet with a piteous whine and movements indicating cruel tortures, and if you should have bread, is it possible that you, having discerned hungry death in its hollow gaze, would not give the bread to it, even if this piece of bread were intended for a completely different use? Thus I beg one word of love from you!..."

In the melodramatic denouement with the primitive contrast of a wedding and a funeral, yet characteristic for Lermontov's tendencies, we again find a phrase from a poem ("The 11th day of June, 1831"): "People are just to the fallen."

In the drama *Two Brothers* the everyday, comic element is weakened; it is restricted to the figure of Prince Ligovsky, who is unimportant to the movement of the drama. On the other hand, the dramatic side is intensified and made more complex. Instead of one hero uttering pathetic speeches and monologues, two brothers hostile to one another are taken here; this is a traditional plot for the German *Sturm und Drang* (Klinger's *Die Zwillinge*, Leisewitz's *Julius von Tarent*), whose development is climaxed by Schiller's *Die Räuber*. It is known that Lermontov was fascinated by *Die Räuber* as early as 1829 (letter to M. A. Shan-Girei). Traces of this fascination are revealed not only in the plot construction and in the choice of characters (a father and two sons), but also in the individual scenes. The third act of Lermontov's drama begins with a scene between the father (the old man Moor in Schiller) and the son Aleksandr (Franz):

> "Aleksandr: Recently you have been, it seems, unusually weak, father.
> Dmitry Petrovich: Old age, brother, old age. It's time, it's time to clear out....
> Yes, you wished to tell me something.
> Aleksandr: Yes, indeed....there is one thing about which I must speak with without fail.
> D.P.: It probably is about interest for the board of guardians....But I don't know whether I have the money...
> Aleksandr: In this case money won't help, father.
> D.P.: Well, what is it?
> Aleksandr: It concerns my brother...
> D.P.: What happened to Yurinka?
> Aleksandr: Don't be frightened, he's healthy and happy.
> D.P.: He hasn't lost at cards?
> Aleksandr: O, no!
> D.P.: Listen, I'm telling you in advance....if you tell me something bad about him...I won't believe it....I know that you don't like him!

91

Aleksandr: Therefore, I can't say anything...and you alone could
restrain him," etc.

Obviously the beginning of *Die Räuber* served as the model for this scene: the scene between old Moor and his son Franz. Both Schiller's Franz and Lermontov's Aleksandr are transformed from ordinary theatrical villains into more complex figures combining villainy and intellect, and their acts are explained by the imperfection of the world or by the malice of others. This tendency has an even more definite character in *Sturm und Drang* dramas: there villains emerge in the role of main heroes, endowed with stormy passions and a terrible strength of will. Self-justification is the basic theme of their speeches. Aleksandr's speeches are the same. At the end of the second act a scene between Aleksandr and Vera is depicted:

"Vera: O, better you should kill me!
Aleksandr: Child, do I really resemble an assassin?...
Vera: You are worse!
Aleksandr: Yes, such has been my fate since birth....Everyone has read in my face some signs of evil attributes which were not there, but which they assumed--and [thus] they were born. I was modest; they cursed me for craftiness, and I became secretive. I sensed good and evil deeply; no one comforted me, everyone insulted me, and I became vindictive. I was sullen, my brother happy and open. I felt myself higher than he; they placed me lower, and I became envious. I was ready to love the entire world; no one loved me, and I learned how to hate....My colorless youth passed in a struggle with fate and society; fearing ridicule, I buried my better feelings in the depths of my heart, and they died there. I became proud, served for a long time, and was passed over. I went out into high society, became skillful in the science of life, and saw how others were happy without artfulness....Despair arose in my breast, not the kind which is healed by the barrel of a pistol, but that despair for which there is no medicine either in this or the future life. Finally I made a final effort: I resolved to find out if but once what it means to be loved...and for that I selected you!"

Of course, Lermontov quickly must have been disappointed in this drama too, but he had to use its material. Indeed, Pincess Vera and her husband, who boasts of his gifts, are transferred from this play into the tale "Princess Ligovskaya" (1836), and Aleksandr's entire tirade cited above is transferred *in toto* into *A Hero of Our Time*, where it is inserted into Pechorin's journal (entry of II June). Pechorin is describing his meeting with Mary after a conversation with Grushnitsky about whether or not she loves him: "'Do I really look like an assassin?...' 'You are worse...' I pondered for a moment and then, adopting a deeply-touched expression, said: 'Yes, such has been my fate since childhood! Everyone read on my face signs of evil attributes which were not

there; but they presumed them--and they were born. I was modest; they accused me of craftiness, and I became secretive,'" etc. Here, too, we encounter the same phenomenon which we observed in the verse. Aleksandr's tirade, which has assumed the character of a formula, proves to be equally
applicable both to himself and to Pechorin.

Besides Schiller, Lermontov is fascinated by Shakespeare too, and he
values in Shakespeare precisely what the German *Sturm und Drang* drama-
tists valued in him: the force of passions, the emotional expressiveness of
language, the sharp contrasts of scenes, etc. It is characteristic that in 1831
more than anything else Lermontov likes *Hamlet*, with his tragic pathos
often expressed in the form of pathetic maxims and aphorisms. In a well -
known letter to M. A. Shan-Girei he "defends Shakespeare's honor" and
presents himself as a Russian opponent of French theatrical traditions: "If
he is great, then it is in *Hamlet*; if he is truly Shakespeare, this boundless
genius penetrating to the heart of man, and to the laws of fate, [this] original, that is inimitable Shakespeare, then it is in *Hamlet*. I will start from the
premise that you have a translation not of Shakespeare, but a translation of
the extremely butchered play of Ducis, who, in order to satisfy stupid rules
and cloying taste of Frenchmen incapable of grasping the sublime, changed the
course of the tragedy and omitted a great many characteristic scenes. Un-
fortunately, these translations are performed in our theaters. True, in our
Hamlet there is no gravedigger scene, and others which I don't recollect. In
English *Hamlet* is written half in prose, half in verse. It is true there is not
that scene when Hamlet is speaking with his mother and she points to the
portrait of his deceased father. On the other hand, at that instant, visible
to Hamlet alone, the king's shade appears dressed as it is in the portrait;
and the prince, [now] gazing at the shade, answers his mother. What a living
contrast, how profound!"

The passion for Shakespeare, which arose on the basis of his attraction
for German *Sturm und Drang* drama, is evident in the drama *The Masquerade*, as already has been noted several times. "Strong passions" are the basic
principle of his dramatic art. Arbenin is not so much an Othello as a paradoxical villain of German drama who appraises all the incidents of his life
on a world scale and in his very crimes looks majestic--not like a criminal,
but like a judge. We find in Arbenin's speeches the same antitheses and pathetic formulae with which Aleksandr expresses himself later in the drama
Two Brothers:

> Но я люблю иначе: я все видел,
> Все перечувствовал, все понял, все узнал;

Любил я часто, чаще ненавидел
И более всего страдал.
Сначала все хотел, потом все презирал я;
То сам себя не понимал я,
То мир меня не понимал.
На жизни я своей узнал печать проклятья
И холодно закрыл объятья
Для чувств и счастия земли...

But I love differently: I have seen everything,
Experienced everything, understood everything,
learned everything;
I have loved often, more often hated
And most of all suffered.
At first I wanted everything, then I despised everything;
Now I did not understand myself,
Now the world did not understand me.
I recognized the stamp of a curse upon my life
And coldly closed my arms
To feelings and earthly happiness...

We find fragments of this self-characterization in the speeches of "The Demon" too (and precisely in the last version): that same paradoxical villain, only transferred from an everyday to an abstract metaphysical plane:

Всегда жалеть и не жалеть,
Все знать, все чувствовать, все видеть,
Стараться все возненавидеть
И все на свете презирать!..
Лишь только божие проклятье
Исполнилось, с того же дня
Природы жаркие объятья
Навек остыли для меня...

Always to regret, and not to desire,
To know everything, feel everything, see everything,
To try to come to hate everything
And despise everything in the world!...
As soon as God's curse
Was fulfilled - since that day
The ardent embraces of Nature
Forever have cooled for me.

Lermontov's very transition from the youthful tragedies in verse (*The*

Spaniards is modelled after Lessing's *Nathan der Weise)* to dramas in prose, then again to verse drama and later again to prose (*Two Brothers*) is characteristic. Lermontov's tendency toward verbal pathos leads to verse drama, where the rhetoric does not appear as melodramatic as in prose since it is motivated by the form of speech itself.[33] Combining an everyday tone with the tone of high tragedy as was done earlier, Lermontov models himself on Griboedov in *The Masquerade*: he introduces witticisms, puns, mass scenes and employs lines of different length as in *Woe from Wit*. However, plot construction causes him trouble because even here, as in the narrative poems, everything is concentrated upon Arbenin's individual maxims and formulae and not at all on the drama's movement per se. All the characters surrounding him possess just as conventional and decorative a character as the narrative and descriptive parts of the narrative poems; they are not fused into the drama and easily can be replaced by any other characters. Thus, in the second version of *The Masquerade* there no longer is a Baroness Shtral, and in her stead another character appears, Olenka, whose role is just as weakly written into the play as that of the baroness. Naturally, with such an essentially monologic character to the play, the denouement especially must have posed difficulties for Lermontov. There is no real dramatic center here; Arbenin has nothing else to add to his speeches, the remaining characters are not linked to him in any special way, and their fate is completely unimportant. A special, new character is imperative, one who could aid in concluding the play: such is the role of the "unknown person." He appears as "Nemesis" and concludes the play with words which motivate his appearance:

> Давно хотел я полной мести, -
> И вот вполне я отомщен!

> For a long time I wished for complete revenge
> And now I have been avenged completely!

However, the very grounds for his revenge are poorly motivated and the figure of the "unknown person" remains enigmatic and half fantastic.

Lermontov's dramatic experiments are interesting as an attempt to go beyond the limits of the lyrical genres. On the basis of Lermontov's poetics in the dramatic form, only an abstract, schematic tragedy could develop -- something like the first plays of Leonid Andreev (*The Life of Man, The Black Masks*) or of Blok. There was no basis for such a style in the Russian theater of the 30s: primitive melodrama rich in plot, vaudeville, and high comedy were the genres which fill the repertoire of that period. Lermon-

95

tov's tragedies remained theoretical experiments which arose on the basis of his searchings in the realm of literary genres. After 1836 he never returns to the drama; his work again is concentrated upon poetry and prose.

Up to this point we have been concerned with those works which became well-known only after Lermontov's death, and a few of them many years afterward (for example, the drama *Two Brothers* was first published only in 1880). Now we will turn to material the majority of which was well-known to Lermontov's contemporaries and entered into the literature of his day as something new and fresh. Among the poems of this new period there are works in which echoes of the youthful lyrics are clearly audible; but Lermontov did not publish works of this type, to all appearances deliberately, and they became known later. Such are: "I look to the future with fear," "She sings and the sounds wane," "I do not wish the world to know," "Do not laugh at my prophetic grief," and "The Agreement." Here we find the familiar formulae and maxims, the emotional intensity familiar in early verse, and the pathetic element. The poem "Do not laugh at my prophetic grief" takes us back to an 1830 poem ("When your friend with prophetic grief"), of which it is a re-working. The poem "The Agreement" (1841, although this date is also doubtful) takes us back to that same year 1830 and the poem "To the charming one."

Even the two narrative poems of this period - "The Novice" and "The Demon" - go back to these youthful experiments. Lermontov perfects in them that style of lyrical "tales" on which he had begun work as early as 1829. "The Novice" is a lyric monologue constructed on the model of the Byron-Zhukovsky's "The Prisoner of Chillon," Kozlov's "The Black Monk" and Podolinsky's "The Beggar." If one takes from "A Confession" (1830), "The Boyar Orsha" (1836), and "The Novice" (1840) passages common to all of them, then Lermontov's basic formal design becomes clear: a design containing no elements of milieu, place of action, time, etc. His idea is to write a narrative poem whose hero, an unfortunate youth in the power of others, utters a passionate speech filled with the emotional formulae of contempt, indignation, pining for freedom, etc. On the path toward the realization of this outline Lermontov first provides a dual motive, combining "The Prisoner of Chillon" and "The Black Monk," and out of this comes a monk languishing in prison for some crime which he has committed ("A Confession"). The place of action is chosen by chance and has no significance; "Guadalquivir," of course, is drawn from literature and is mentioned only in the first chapter ("Eddying ran the Guadalquivir"). The hermit's crime is only hinted at:

Таков был рок! Зачем, за что?
Не-знал и знать не мог никто.
. . . .
Пусть монастырский ваш закон
Рукою неба утвержден,
Но в этом сердце есть другой,
Ему не менее святой.
Он оправдал меня, - один
Он сердца полный властелин.

. . . .
Забудь, что жил я...что любил
Гораздо более, чем жил...
Кого любил? Отец святой,
Вот что умрет во мне, со мной!
За жизнь, за мир, за небо вам
Я тайны этой не продам!

        Such was fate! Why, for what purpose?
        No one could and did not know.
        . . . .
        Let your monastic law
        Be confirmed by heaven's hand,
        Yet in this heart there is another
        No less sacred to it.
        It justified me, alone
        It is the complete master of my heart.
        . . . .
        Forget that I lived... that I loved
        Much more than I lived...
        Whom did I love - Holy Father
        This is what will die in me, with me!
        For life, for the world, for heaven
        I will not sell you this secret!

Like the original draft, "A Confession" still has a wholly schematic character. The outline still has acquired neither plot nor decoration. The basic verse (rhythmic-syntactic) formulae have been formulated, but the general plan is too bare and abstract. Already in 1831 Lermontov returns to this plan and, wishing to flesh it out with his material, notes: "Write the notes of a young 17-year old monk. He has been in a monastery since childhood; he has not read other than sacred books. A passionate soul is languishing. Ideals." As is evident from this notation, the motif of a crime, which is introduced so weakly into "A Confession" in order to place the hero in prison, fades away: the monastery must play the role of a prison. From here the path to "The Novice" is direct; but in the interval between these forms the narrative poem undergoes yet one more transformation linked with the tendency toward the "historical" narrative poem. From the shores of the Guadalquivir, which laves the first two lines of "A Confession" and then immediately disappears from the scene, the action is transferred to 16th - century Moscow:

> Во время оно жил да был
> В Москве боярин Михаил,
> Прозваньем Орша-Важный сан
> Дал Орше Грозный Иоанн
>
> и т. д.

> At that time there lived
> In Moscow a boyar Mikhail
> Nicknamed Orsha. Ivan the Terrible
> Gave Orsha an important office
> etc.

New characters appear around the central hero. He himself is a monk who has fled from a monastery. The situation of "A Confession" (monk and prisoner) is repeated, but the crime is no longer a mystery and the monasticism is removed to the past.

The abstract plot of "A Confession" is developed by descriptive and narrative material. At the beginning of the second chapter there is a scene near the monastery, after that a refectory with a detailed description of its furnishings; only after this does Arseny's speech begin, in which we recognize the words of the Spanish hermit:

> Ты слушать исповедь мою
> Сюда пришел! - благодарю.
> Не понимаю, что была
> У вас за мысль? - мои дела
> И без меня ты должен знать,
> А душу можно ль рассказать?
>
> и т. д.

> You came here to hear
> My confession, and I thank you.
> I do not understand what thought
> You entertained? My affairs
> You must know even without me,
> But is it possible to relate one's soul?
> etc.

The text of "A Confession" went into "The Boyar Orsha" almost in its entirety and was expanded in volume. We learn from Arseny's speech that he was taken by Orsha and "from early years placed under the strict supervision of monks":

> И вырос в тесных я стенах,
> Душой дитя,- судьбой монах!

> And I grew up within narrow walls
> In soul a child, - by fate a monk.

A portion of the notation cited above is realized here. Later Arseny flees from the monastery; this tale grants Lermontov an opportunity to introduce a number of new lyric formulae. Among them there is one which takes us back to the year 1830, where the poem "The Cross on a Cliff" concludes with the lines:

> О, если б взойти удалось мне туда,
> Как я бы молился и плакал тогда;
> И после я сбросил бы цепь бытия
> И с бурею братом назвался бы я! -

> O, if I could succeed in ascending there
> How then I should pray and weep;
> And afterward I would cast off the chain of existence
> And call myself brother to the storm.

In "The Boyar Orsha":

> Боязнь с одеждой кинул прочь,
> Благословил и хлад и ночь,
> Забыл печали бытия
> И бурю братом назвал я.

> I cast off fear with my clothes,
> I blessed both the cold and the night,
> I forgot the sadnessess of life
> And called the storm brother.

Somewhat altered, this was transferred into "The Novice":

> О! я как брат

99

Обняться с бурей был бы рад!

O! I would be glad to embrace
The storm like a brother!

A formula is worked into the end of "The Boyar Orsha," which we find also in an early sketch of "The Demon" and in "Vadim"; it is one of Lermontov's typical poetic saws:

Что без нее земля и рай?
Одни лишь звучные слова,
Блестящий храм - без божества!....

What are the earth and paradise without her?
Nothing but sonorous words,
A glittering temple without a divinity!

In "The Demon," 1833:

Мой рай, мой ад в твоих очах.
Я проклял прошлую беспечность;
С тобою розно мир и вечность -
Пустые звучные слова,
Прекрасный храм без божества.

My paradise, my hell are in your eyes.
I cursed past carelessness;
With you peace and eternity are two different things -
Empty sonorous words,
A beautiful temple without a divinity.

In "Vadim":

,,Мир без тебя, что такое?... храм без божества..."

"What is the world without you?...
a temple without a divinity..."

2

However, the narrative poem in a new form also could not satisfy Lermontov. On the one hand, Arseny's speech suppresses the entire "situational" part of the poem; there is no real link per se in it with the national and historical coloration to which so much space was devoted at the beginning. On the other hand, the poem's end (Orsha's death and the frightful spectacle of his deceased daughter under lock and key) weakens the force of the basic scene (Arseny's speech) and makes of it an episode. It is natural that Lermontov returns to the narrative poem once more and precisely to his original plan, where the hero must be the sole center and his passionate speech the basic content. Motivation by means of a crime, and the hero's love connected with it, prove to be unnecessary; a monastery was sufficient for the lyric tale as conceived, and it had to be firmly established as the main motivating force. The action is transferred to Georgia;[34] this grants an opportunity to develop the decorative portion, while not introducing any unnecessary historical and national material. Georgia appears as something intrinsically poetic, as an exotic element which does not require special motivation. After innumerable Caucasian poems and tales had made the Caucasus a fixed literary decoration (which Tolstoy later destroyed with such irony), there was no need to motivate the choice of Georgia. Thus out of 'The Boyar Orsha" comes "The Novice," in which, other than the two introductory chapters, all that remains up to the end takes the form of the uninterrupted "confession" of a monk. Furthermore, the motif of a crime has been dropped because it not only did not aid but even hindered the development of the basic idea: an extended confession in the presence of judges would have looked like a contradiction or an incongruity. In "The Boyar Orsha" Arseny's speech had to be interrupted with the rejoinders of Orsha, the Father Superior, and the monk, in order to impart to it the character of answers to questions. In the new form the hero's speech is a genuine confession; it does not occur prior to an execution, as in the early poem, but simply prior to death. The attempt to fill the outline with a well-developed plot ("The Boyar Orsha") was unsuccessful;[35] perhaps it was prompted by the dramatic and narrative experiments which coincide in time with work on "The Boyar Orsha" (*The Masquerade,* "Princess Ligovskaya"). Lermontov returns to the lyric style, to the monologue form of Kozlov's "The Black Monk," apparently not by accident. This can be established with particular confidence in regard to the motivation of the flight from the monastery. We read in "The Black Monk":

Но умереть хотелось мне
В моей родимой стороне.
Я стал скучать в горах чужбины;
На рощи наши, на долины

Хотел последний бросить взгляд.

> But I wished to die
> In my native land.
> I began to be bored in foreign mountains:
> I wished to cast a last glance
> At our groves and valleys.

Incidentally, we encounter the same motif also in Podolinsky's "The Beggar," a motif traditionally linked to the theme of a "prisoner":

> Далеко родина моя!
> Ее давно покинул я -
> Давно!... но душу старика
> Томит по родине тоска!
> О, если б мне, когда-нибудь,
> Опять на милую взглянуть!
> . . . .
> И в той далекой стороне
> Могилы есть, родные мне;
> Близ них и я, когда бы мог,
> Легко б на вечный отдых лег;
> . . . .
> И я бы снова, может быть,
> Хотел отчизну разлюбить,
> Но, как по вольности, о ней
> Тоска живет в груди моей!

> My homeland is far away!
> I left it long ago -
> Long ago!...but yearning for this homeland
> Wearies an old man's soul!
> O, if I but sometime
> Again could glance at my beloved!
> . . . .
> And in that distant land
> There are graves dear to me;
> Near them I too, if I could,
> Would easily lie down to eternal rest.
> . . . .
> And again I, perhaps, would wish
> To cease loving my native land,
> But, involuntarily, yearning
> For her lives in my breast!

"The Novice" is linked to Podolinsky's poem not so much on the level of plot as on the verse (rhythmic-syntactic) and stylistic plane. Literary kinship is evident not only (and often not as much) in the purely verbal sphere, as much as in the character of verse phrasing and rhythmic-syntactic construction. In the verse line, due to the unity and compactness of the rhythmic line,[36] syntactic constructions appear as if freshly invented, even those most used in ordinary speech. The verse line employed by Podolinsky in "The Beggar" and by Lermontov in "The Novice." (and earlier in "A Confession" and "The Boyar Orsha"), and which goes back to Zhukovsky's "The Prisoner of Chillon" (iambic tetrameter with adjacent masculine rhymes), is marked by particular compactness: phrases in this verse line split up into short units which quickly displace one another and form a chain of small links. Characteristic of this verse line are both strong *enjambements* which connect the short phrase units, and a special intensity of words standing at the end. Therefore, each word here acquires a special rhythmic-semantic weight, while the rhymes stand out due to their rhythmic-syntactic intensity. This is why the reader of "The Novice" is struck by its affinity with "The Prisoner of Chillon" and "The Beggar," although one could point to only a few simple lexical correspondences.[37] Such lines from "The Novice" as

> Хотя на миг, когда-нибудь,
> Мою пылающую грудь
> . . . .
> Мне было весело вдохнуть
> В мою измученную грудь

> If but for an instant sometime
> My flaming breast
> . . . . . .
> I was happy to breathe
> Into my tormented breast

remind us of Podolinsky's lines ("Oh, if I but sometime," "In my yearning breast," "His tormented breast/Now again could breathe") precisely because in this line the word "sometime," as a rhyme for the word "breast," acquires the force of a verse formula irrespective of the semantic closeness of the entire phrase. And the construction "Into my tormented breast," does not look like an ordinary utterance, but rather like a verse formula. It is the same with such formations as:

> Я вышел из лесу. И вот

Проснулся день и хоровод
Светил напутственных исчез
и т. д.

> I came out of the forest. *And suddenly*
> The day awoke and the round-dance
> Of parting stars disappeared
> etc.

In Podolinsky:

Я ничего не знал... но вот
Однажды, слышу я, падет
Затвор с дверей моих
и т. д.

> I knew nothing... *but suddenly*
> Once, I hear, falling
> The bar of my doors
> etc.

Lermontov intensifies the rhythmic-syntactic meaning of the rhymes even more by often employing not binary, but ternary and even quaternary rhymes, such as:

И смутно понял я тогда,
Что мне на родину следа
Не проложить уж никогда.
. . . .
Ко мне он кинулся на грудь,
Но в горло я успел воткнуть
И там два раза повернуть
Мое ружье . . . .
. . . .
И как они навстречу дню
Я поднял голову мою.....
Я осмотрелся; не таю,
Мне стало страшно: на краю
Грозящей бездны я лежал,
Где выл, крутясь, сердитый вал;
Туда вели ступени скал,

Но лишь злой дух по ним шагал
и т. д.

And I understood vaguely then
That I would never trace
My way back to my homeland.
. . . .
He threw himself upon my breast
But I succeeded in plunging into his throat
And twice there twisting
My weapon . . . .
. . . .
And like them, towards the day
I raised my head . . . .
I looked around; I do not conceal
That I was frightened: on the edge
Of a threatening abyss I lay,
Where, swirling, an angry billow howled;
The cliff steps led there
But only an evil spirit had trodden them.
etc.

Two-line phrases with a strong division between them (with masculine rhyme) likewise are very characteristic for the verse line of "The Novice." It is precisely this which imbues the entire poem with a special vocal intensity and abruptness: a phrase is not pronounced all at once, rather in two segments:

Я молод, молод...... Знал ли ты
Разгульной юности мечты?
Или не знал, или забыл,
Как ненавидел и любил;
. . . .
Ты слушать исповедь мою
Сюда пришел, благодарю.
Все лучше перед кем-нибудь
Словами облегчить мне грудь.
. . . .
Я знал одной лишь думы власть, -
Одну, - но пламенную страсть:
Она как червь во мне жила,
Изгрызла душу и сожгла.

I am young, young... Have you known
The dreams of wild youth?
Either you have not known or have forgotten
How you hated and loved;
. . . .
You came here to listen
To my confession, I thank you.
It is always better in someone's presence
To lighten my breast with words.
. . . .
I have known the power of only one solitary thought
Known one, but ardent passion:
It lived in me like a worm,
It gnawed and consumed my soul.

We find the same in Podolinsky's "The Beggar":

И в той далекой стороне
Могилы есть, родные мне;
Близь них и я, когда бы мог,
Легко б на вечный отдых лег;
Но для меня тот чудный край
Закрыт, как и небесный рай,
И даже плакать я о нем
Не смею в сиротстве моем!
. . . .
Но понял я, какую власть
Взяла над сердцем эта страсть,
И с этой страстью, видит бог,
Хотел бороться и не мог!

And in that distant land
There are graves dear to me;
Near them, I too, if I could,
Easily would lie down to eternal rest;
But for me that marvelous realm
Is closed, as is heavenly paradise,
And I dare not even weep for it
In my orphanhood!
. . . .
But I understood what power
This passion held over my heart,
And with that passion, as God is my witness,
I wished but could not struggle!

106

In such a rhythmic-syntactic system each departure from the limits of a two-line phrase is felt as a strong verse device; and Lermontov repeatedly employs it, extending periods by interpolating appositions, and increasing the impression of a developing phrase by means of ternary rhymes and *enjambements:*

Теперь один старик седой,
Развалин страж полуживой,
Людьми и смертию забыт,
Сметает пыль с могильных плит,
Которых надпись говорит
О славе прошлой....
. . . .
Внизу глубоко подо мной
Поток, усиленной грозой,
Шумел, и шум его глухой,
Сердитых сотне голосов
Подобился . . . .

Now a grey old man alone,
The half-live guardian of ruins,
Forgotten by people and by death,
Sweeps dust from the gravestones,
Whose inscriptions speak
Of past glory . . . .
. . . .
Below, deep beneath me
A stream, swelled by a storm,
Stirred noisily, and its hollow noise,
A hundred angry voices
Resembled . . .

Similar periods are closed by a new short formula which is notable for its energy. Almost every chapter concludes with such a heightening (*pointe*):

Я эту страсть во тьме ночной
Вскормил слезами и тоской,
Ее пред небом и землей
Я ныне громко признаю
И о прощеньи не молю. -
. . . .
И я, как жил, в земле чужой

Умру рабом и сиротой.

. . . .

Тебе есть в мире что забыть,
Ты жил - я также мог бы жить!

. . . .

Воспоминанья тех минут
Во мне, со мной пускай умрут.

> This passion in the dark of night I
> Fed with tears and anguish;
> Before heaven and earth
> I now loudly acknowledge it
> And do not pray for forgiveness.
> . . . .
> And I, as I lived, in a foreign land
> Will die a slave and an orphan.
> . . . .
> You have something to forget in the world,
> You have lived - I likewise could have lived!
> . . . .
> Memories of those minutes
> Let them die in me, with me.

"The Novice" as a whole marks the completion of those experiments in the emotional-monologic narrative poem which Lermontov had begun while still a youth. Neither in the history of his creative activity nor in the history of Russian poetry does "The Novice" appear as a new genre, and it does not open up a new path.[38] On the contrary, it is a last word, a summing-up of the development of the Russian lyrical narrative poem, incorporating the experiments of Zhukovsky, Kozlov, Podolinsky, and others. We have seen that in the sphere of the narrative poem Lermontov does not break with his own past, and only perfects what he had adumbrated as far back as 1830.

The same should be said about "The Demon." Lermontov's "The Demon" is a composite narrative poem which incorporated Russian and Western material and completed the development of the Russian narrative (lyrico - epic) poem coming from Pushkin. The introduction of historical and national material also interested Pushkin; sometimes (as in "The Prisoner of the Caucasus") it came to the fore and suppressed the lyrical or plot basis. In Lermontov all material is conventional, decorative. In this respect "The Demon" is a typical literary oleograph. Zhukovsky, Pushkin, Polezhaev, Kozlov, Podolinsky, on the one hand, and on the other Byron, Moore, Lamartine, and Alfred de Vigny, all are united in "The Demon." In the initial sketches the poem is wholly abstract; there is no time, no place of action, and no names.

Cliffs, a sea, even an ocean - such is the setting. In one passage a "Spanish Lute" is mentioned, but precisely why it is Spanish remains unknown. Already in this period the idea of an everyday background appears in Lermontov. There is a plot notation: "During the Jewish captivity in Babylon (from the Bible). A Jewess. A blind father. He[39] sees her sleeping for the first time. Later she sings to her father about olden times, and about the angel's nearness - *as before*. The Jew returns to his homeland. Her grave remains in the foreign land." (*As before* is evidently a reference to the nun's song in an 1830 sketch ("Like a sail over the sea's abyss" etc.). In the history of the creation of "The Demon," as in the history of "The Novice," an abstract sketch exists independently of the material; the material is in a process of selection. It is impossible to imagine Pushkin's narrative poem in a different setting; the material itself is so much a part of the form. In Lermontov this organic link, this mutual interweaving of form and material, does not exist.

I will not compare "The Demon" with Moore's "The Love of the Angels" or with Alfred de Vigny's "Eloa." This has already been done more than once;[40] it is perfectly clear here that it is not a question of any "influence" or "congeniality," but of the simple use of ready-made material. On the one hand, someone else's plot is decked out with the exoticism traditional for the Russian narrative poem; on the other hand, it is made more complex by means of ordinary lyric formulae and maxims (it is given a *pointe).* On Russian soil, other than a link with the epos of the Middle Ages and the narrative poem in the style of Milton, this plot lost its splendor, its theological philosophicalness, and became much more primitive. Out of the Satan of the West came the "melancholy demon," in whom are visible features of the paradoxical villains familiar to us if only from Lermontov's dramas, like Arbenin in *The Masquerade.* This time he is masked as a Demon because in this situation he is free from any motivation and requires neither special rehabilitation nor special "retribution." On the other hand, Lermontov could not hold out on the chill height of the abstract metaphysical poem. He sensed the need to make the narrative poem more domestic or "comfortable," in the end concentrating the action in a corner of that same Georgia where the unfortunate monk from "A Confession" had also taken refuge. Of course, here Georgia is just as conventional and operatically decorative as it had been in "The Novice." It is utterly unlike Petersburg in Pushkin's "The Bronze Horseman" or the Ukraine in his "Poltava." The landscape is marked by general features, and it is characteristic that among its details borrowings also occur. For example, the lines "The breathing of a thousand plants/And the voluptuous heat of mid-day" evidently originate in T. Moore's poem ("The Loves of the Angels") where we find: "The silent breathing of the flowers -

The melting light that beam'd above." In view of the general lowering of the plot, the role of the angel became quite insignificant and seems prompted not so much by artistic as by moral considerations. His speech at the end of the poem ("Disappear, gloomy spirit of doubt") is one of its most risky passages, standing almost on the boundary of the comic.

As in Lermontov's previous poems, "The Demon" is saturated with all kinds of lyric formulae, antitheses, and so on. Again, almost every chapter has its *pointe;* furthermore, some of them are taken from old material and some are borrowed from other authors. Chapter III concludes with a quote from Pushkin's "The Prisoner of the Caucasus" which looks almost parodic here:[41]

> И дик и чуден был вокруг
> Весь божий мир: -- но гордый дух
> Презрительным окинул оком
> Творенье бога своего,
> <u>И на челе его высоком</u>
> <u>Не отразилось ничего.</u>

> And wild and beautiful around was
> All God's world: but the proud spirit
> Cast a contemptuous eye
> On the creation of his God
> *And on his high brow*
> *Nothing was reflected.*

Chapter IV ends with a formula which is familiar to us both from the lyric poetry and *The Masquerade,* and it already sounds like a saying:

> И все, что пред собой он видел,
> Он презирал, иль ненавидел.

> And everything that he saw before him
> He despised or hated.

Chapter VII, properly speaking, consists entirely of one rhetorical formula on the theme -

> Клянусь, красавица такая
> Под солнцем юга не цвела.

> I swear such a beauty

110

Did not blossom under the southern sun.

At the end of Chapter VIII we find a formula familiar to us from two poems of 1832 and 1837:

> Однако все ее движенья,
> Улыбки, речи и черты
> Так полны жизни, вдохновенья,
> Так полны чудной простоты.
> ("Она не гордой красотою" 1832 г.)

> However, all her movements
> Smiles, speeches and features
> Are so full of life, of inspiration
> So full of wonderful simplicity.
> ("Not by proud beauty does she," 1832)

> Идет ли - все ее движенья,
> Иль молвит слово - все черты
> - Так полны чувства, выраженья,
> Так полны дивно простоты!
> ("Она поет - и звуки тают" 1837 г.)

> Whether she walks or utters a word,
> All her movements, all her features
> Are so full of feeling, of expression
> So wonderfully full of simplicity.
> ("She sings - and the sounds wane," 1837)

In "The Demon" we read:

> И были все ее движенья
> Так стройны, полны выраженья,
> Так полны милой простоты,
> Что если б Демон, пролетая,
> В то время на нее взглянул,
> То, прежних братий вспоминая,
> Он отвернулся б - и вздохнул. . .

> All her movements were
> So harmonious, full of expression,
> So full of sweet simplicity,
> That if the Demon, winging by,
> Had glanced at her at that time,
> Then recalling former brotherhoods

111

He would have turned away - and sighed . . .

Chapter IX concludes with a typical formula-*pointe*:

Забыть? - забвенья не дай бог: -
Да он и не взял бы забвенья! . . . . .

> Forget? May God not grant oblivion: -
> And he would not have accepted oblivion! . . .

The end of chapter XVI - "He was like a clear evening: Neither day, nor night, nor gloom, nor light" - is reminiscent of the lines from "The Prisoner of Chillon":

То не было ни ночь, ни день,
Ни тяжкий свет тюрьмы моей
и т. д.

> It was neither night nor day,
> Nor the harsh light of my prison
> etc.

The Demon's first speech concludes with a traditional saying, which already has been spoken about above:

Что без тебя мне эта вечность?
Моих владений бесконечность?
Пустые звучные слова,
Обширный храм - без божества!

> What is this eternity to me without you?
> The endlessness of my domains?
> Empty sonorous words,
> A vast temple-without a divinity!

The Demon's "vow" is an extended rhetorical formula (its prototype is in Alfred de Vigny's "Eloa"), which is constructed as if by itself, mechanically, by means of an uninterrupted formation of antitheses: the first day - the last day; the shame of a crime - the triumph of truth; the bitter torment of a fall - the brief dream of victory; a meeting - a parting; heaven - hell; a last glance - a first tear; bliss - suffering.

As in "The Novice," "The Demon" arose from an abstract plan in which there was no place for any national or historical material; the exotic

112

element appeared later. The initial plan (1829) is an outline where, instead of Tamara, "a mortal" figures, and where the Demon's struggle with the Angel possesses great significance: "The Demon learns that the angel loves a mortal. The Demon learns her identity and tempts her so that she forsakes the angel, but soon dies and becomes a spirit of hell. The Demon tempted her, saying that God is unjust and other of his truths..." In this form the poem would have been very close to Western treatments of the plot; of course, the plan was inspired by them. If one considers the above-cited notation, where the mortal is transformed into a Jewess ("During the Jewish captivity in Babylon"), as a project coming after 1830, then one can assert that already at this time Lermontov is beginning to seek out some everyday material for his plan and for the verse lines at hand. For an abstract metaphysical poem of the kind which apparently Lermontov conceived for his future "The Demon," there were not sufficiently strong traditions in Russian poetry. The Russian epic narrative poem had taken shape as a poem with either exotic descriptive material (like Pushkin's "The Prisoner of the Caucasus" and "The Gypsies") or national-historical material ("Poltava," "The Bronze Horseman"). Thus, an abstract narrative poem about a Demon and a mortal is transformed into a poem-legend about the Georgian princess Tamara, where the combination characteristic of "The Novice" recurs in a more complex form: the combination of intense rhetoric originating in "The Prisoner of Chillon" with the decorativeness recalling Podolinsky's narrative poems. A new genre did not emerge because no sharp departure from traditions occurred either in the material or in the composition; but with regard to style, the traditional lyrico-epic poem acquired that dramatic force and vigor of expression which had been lacking in the narrative poems of Zhukovsky, Kozlov, and Podolinsky.

In the language of "The Demon" there is neither the simplicity nor the sharp precision with which Pushkin's narrative poems sparkle, but there is that brilliance of emotional rhetoric which had to arise on the ruins of the Classical age of Russian verse. Lermontov writes in formulae which apparently hypnotize even him; he no longer senses in them semantic nuances and details; for him they exist as abstract speech formations, as fusions of words, and not as their "linkages." The general emotional effect is important to him; apparently he postulates a rapid reader, who will not linger over semantic or syntactic details but will only seek an impression of the whole. The semantic basis of words and verbal combinations begins to dull, but then their declamatory (sound and emotional) coloration begins to glitter with unprecedented sparkle. This shift in the very nature of poetic language constitutes the main peculiarity, the strength and the essence of Lermontov's poetics; it is a transference of dominance from effects characteristic only of spoken verse to effects characteristic of melodious and declamatory verse. Precisely here is concealed the reason for his attraction to lyric formulae and his attitude toward them as cliches worked out once and for all. From here, too, comes the strangeness of some of Lermontov's turns of speech and combinations; the emotional hypnosis of his speech is so strong that it is easy to pass over them. But once we stop, we are often perplexed by them. I already have indicated above the contamination of the expressions "superfluous *guest at a feast*" and "unnecessary *member of existense*" into one: "unnecessary *member at a feast*." The initial formula of "The Demon," which was composed by Lermontov in the very first sketch and proceeded unchanged up to the last, is typical of Lermontov's language: "A mournful Demon, *spirit of exile*." By analogy with Pushkin's "spirit of *negation*, spirit of *doubt*," something not wholly intelligible arises: "a spirit of *exile*" - is this an *exiled* spirit or an *exiling* spirit? Neither one nor the other. It is a verbal fusion in which the stress falls on the word "*exile*." and the whole represents an emotional formula. The path to this combination was broken by Podolinsky in the narrative poem *Div i Peri*:[42] his expression "a gloomy spirit of solitude" ("pensive and sad") stands on the boundary between Pushkin and Lermontov. As Strakhov already has hinted, the Demon's entire vow is just such an emotional-rhetorical fusion. In general the Demon's speech advances by means of emotional antitheses, repetitions, parallelisms and formulae, which exert an influence through their rhythmic-intonational vigor:

Я бич рабов моих земных,
Я царь познанья и свободы,
Я враг небес, я зло природы.
И, видишь, я у ног твоих!
Тебе принес я в умиленье
Молитву тихую любви,
Земное первое мученье
И слезы первые мои.
. . . .
Люблю тебя не здешней страстью,
Как полюбить не можешь ты:
Всем упоением, всей властью
Бессмертной мысли и мечты.
. . . .
Всегда жалеть, и не желать,

Все знать, все чувствовать, все видеть,
Стараться все возненавидеть,
И все на свете презирать!..

> *I* am the *scourge* of my earthly slaves,
> *I* am the *tsar* of knowledge and freedom,
> *I* am the *enemy* of heaven, *I* am the *evil* of nature,
> And, you see, I am at your feet!
> I have brought you in tenderness
> A quiet prayer of love
> The *first* earthly torment
> And my *first* tears.
> . . . .
> I love you with a love not of this earth,
> As you cannot love;
> With *all* the ecstasy, with *all* the power
> Of an immortal thought and dream.
> . . . .
> Always *to regret* and not *to desire*
> *To know everything, to feel everything, to see everything,*
> *To try to conceive a hatred for everything,*
> *And to despise everything in the world!...*

The last example also is very typical of Lermontov's verse language: it is an emotional fusion and at the same time an abstract outline, an algebraic formula. The "regret-desire" antithesis is not a semantic one (its sense even remains not altogether clear), but an emotional-phonic one; it is a kind of pun in which the word "desire" *(zhelat')* did not arise as a semantic "link-age" but as a sound gesture. Further, we have a syntactic construction whose rhythmic-intonational strength suppresses the semantic base. Is that "and" ("And to despise everything in the world") a simple coordinating conjunction so that the verb "to try" governs both sentences equally, or does this "and" stand for "and meanwhile," in which case the verb "to despise" is not subordinated to the verb "to try"? The first interpretation may seem simpler and more natural but, on the other hand, the initial antithesis inclines toward the latter, where "and" has precisely this second meaning and requires its intonational repetition. The second interpretation is suggested also by the use of a similar formula in "Vadim" where its meaning is somewhat clearer: "I wished to conceive a hatred for humanity - and *against my will* I began to despise it" (chapter VIII). The rhythmic-syntactic plan dominates the verbal material and suppresses it. That equilibrium between the verse line and the word, so characteristic of Pushkin, is violated. In the

115

words of I. Aksakov, the poetry ceases to be "sincere." Lermontov's attraction to rhythmic-intonational and emotional effect is expressed not only in the repetitions and the very choice of epithets and set phrases, but also in the accumulation of fixed verse forms. Lines of the type "inexplicable anxiety" (which runs through Podolinsky - compare his narrative poem "Borsky"), where the rhythmic intensity is maintained by the emotional intensity and results in an intensification of the intonational emphasis, occur throughout the text of "The Demon" like a fixed verse device:

И Демон видел . . . . . . На мгновенье
Неизъяснимое волненье
В себе почувствовал он вдруг.
Немой души его пустыню
Наполнил благодатный звук, -
И вновь постигнул он святыню
Любви, добра и красоты . . . . . [43]
. . . .
Она, вскочив, глядит вокруг . . . .
Невыразимое смятенье
                              и т. д.
. . . .
Меня терзает дух лукавый
Неотразимою мечтой;
. . . .
Поныне возле кельи той
Насквозь прожженный видень камень
Слезою жаркою как пламень,
Не человеческой слезой!. . . .
. . . .
Спастись от думы неизбежной
И незабвенное забыть!
. . . .
Надежд погибших и страстей
Несокрушимый мавзолей.
. . . .
Ее душа была из тех,
Которых жизнь одно мгновенье
Невыносимого мученья,
Недосягаемых утех.

And the Demon saw..... For a moment
He suddenly felt in himself
Inexplicable anxiety.
An abundant sound filled
The desert of his mute soul
And again he reached the sacred shrine
Of love, goodness, and beauty.....

. . . .

Leaping up she looks around ...
Inexpressible confusion
              etc.

. . . .

The cunning spirit torments me
With an *irresistible* dream;

. . . .

Until now near that cell
A stone is visible burned through
By a tear hot as a flame,
Not a human tear! ...

. . . .

Escape from the unavoidable thought
And forget the **unforgettable**

. . . .

The *indestructible* mausoleum
Of lost hopes and passions.

. . . .

Her soul was one of those
Whose life is a single moment
Of *unbearable* torment,
Unattainable pleasures.

In Pushkin the same rhythmic device ("magnificent carpets," "in noisily broad [*shirokoshumnye*] groves") has another stylistic meaning because the epithets retain their independent meaning, and that is why the combination itself does not change into an emotional fusion but remains a semantic "linkage."[44]

Thus, in "The Demon" as in "The Novice," Lermontov fulfilled those stylistic intentions which are rooted in his youthful experiments: indeed, he "got rid of" these persistent plans, after having achieved through great effort a kind of formulation of them in which the basic tendencies of his style found sufficiently vivid and complete expression. The traditional Russian narrative poem appeared in a new guise--aiming at declamation and decorativeness, emphasizing emotional expressiveness, rhetoric, the "memorability" of lyrical formulae. As a result, the form disintegrated, the genre turned into a schema and the Russian lyrico-epic narrative poem had run its course.

In analyzing Lermontov's youthful lyrics I have already noted the absence of classical genres. The boundary sharply dividing two contiguous generations lies somewhere between the years 1825 and 1830. We find both odes and epistles still in Ryleev and Polezhaev, but they have already disappeared in Lermontov, as have classical elegies. The lyric genres are losing their definition and are blending with one another. In Lermontov's poetry of 1836-1841 one can observe a vacillation between various styles and genres, and attempts to combine them. The initial fascination with the English verse line (pauses and iambic pentameter with masculine rhymes) and the forms of the Byronic lyric (like the poem "The llth day of June, 1831") passes, and Lermontov returns to Russian traditions. By-passing Pushkin, whose poetry at this time was no longer satisfying and had begun to be perceived as belonging to "yesterday," Lermontov settles on Zhukovsky and the poets of his school. He makes this tradition more complex by means of stylistic devices which, prior to him, had been adumbrated in the lyric poetry of such poets as Ryleev, Polezhaev, A. Odoevsky, and others. These poets united chiefly around Griboedov (the Griboedov group), and had been pushed to the background by the development and influence of Pushkin and his coterie. This combination, too, imparts to Lermontov's lyric poetry that "eclectic" character about which Kyukhelbeker spoke. Alongside the ballad and the meditation, such as "When the yellowing cornfield waves" or "I set off alone upon the road," there are poems in an oratorical, declamatory style (like the poem on Pushkin's death, like "Meditation," "The lst of January," "The Last Housewarming," etc.) in which one can recognize the old "oratorical" tradition of the ode running through the poetry of Ryleev, Polezhaev, etc. And alongside works of a melodious style where lyric intonation or verse melody serve as the dominant element, we find vivid examples of a rhetorical style where oratorical intonation dominates, and where speech movement is determined by declamatory contrasts. Lermontov revives Zhukovsky's "captivating sweetness," which the latter's epigones had exaggerated to a cloying sweetness, and imparts a new taste to it by mixing it with a slight dose of bitter alcohol. A heavy-headed intoxication results from this, but it was necessary to the age. The intoxication of the Pushkin verse line already seemed too weak, too ethereal; a need for special spices arose.

In the interval between 1832 and 1835 Lermontov writes his erotic narrative poems: "The Hospital," "A Holiday at Peterhof," and "The Uhlan's Wife." The influence of the Pushkin verse line found a haven here (for example, the description of Peterhof). However, whereas Pushkin's eroticism did not represent any deviation or inconsistency and passed easily into the general system of his creative work, Lermontov's erotica creates the impression of some temporary binge and possesses not so much an erotic as a pornographic character. Eroticism is distinguished from pornography in that it finds witty allegories and puns for the most candid situations and it is this which lends it literary value. Since poetry in general is almost wholly the art of speaking allegorically, in order to make palpable the very matter of the word in all its attributes, it is thus perfectly understandable that an erotic theme, as a forbidden theme possessing no canonized poetic *topoi* for its expression, interests the poet as a purely literary, stylistic problem. Such is the case with Voltaire's "Pucelle" or Pushkin's "Gavriiliada." This is not at all the case in Lermontov: instead of allegories and puns in his verse we see simply scabrous terminology whose coarseness produces no impression because it is not an artistic device (as does the unexpected crude oath, for example, in Pushkin's poem "The Wagon of Life," where it functions comically because it occurs as a result of the development of a profound metaphor). It is no accident that Lermontov wrote these poems precisely in that period when his creative work, very intense and prolific at the beginning (1830-1831), suddenly weakened and almost stopped. Disappointment in his youthful work and gloomy thoughts of insignificance apparently are concealed behind these poems. There are hints of this in the letters of 1832-1833: "a secret awareness that I shall end life as an insignificant person tortures me...I don't know why, the poetry of my soul has been extinguished... I am writing little, reading not much more; my novel[45] is a total despair... I can not imagine what impression my important news will produce upon you: until now I have lived for a literary career, I have brought so many sacrifices to my ungrateful idol and now I am a warrior. Perhaps this is the particular will of Providence; perhaps this path is the shortest one, and if it does not lead me to my first goal, perhaps it may not lead me to the final goal of all that exists: to die from a bullet in the chest is in no way worse than dying from the slow agony of old age... alas ! the time of my dreams has passed; there is faith no more; I need sensual delights, tactile happiness, such happiness as is purchased with gold, so that I could carry it with me in my pocket, like a snuff-box, only so that it might tempt my sensibilities, leaving my soul in peace and idleness!" Even if a significant portion of these reports must be acknowledged as literary stylization, all the same an element of actuality must remain in them; in the given instance this element interests me because I am inclined to view these same poems of 1833-1834 not as literary works but as a psychological document justifying the division of Lermontov's creative activity into two periods (1829 -

119

1832 and 1836-1841).

A new period of creative activity is revealed in his work on "The Boyar Orsha." Work on lyric poetry resumes and gradually increases. In 1836 Lermontov still is moving slowly and gropingly, testing various genres and styles. "The Dying Gladiator," "The Mermaid," "A Jewish Melody," "In the Album" ("Like a solitary tomb"), and "A Branch of Palestine": here is the entire output for 1836. The poem "In the Album" is an adaptation (an approximation of Byron's original) of an 1830 poem of the same title ("No, I do not demand attention"). "The Dying Gladiator"[46] is an experiment in the declamatory style something like a political ode, especially if one takes note of the poem's end: it is crossed out in the manuscript but apparently with an eye to the censor and not for artistic considerations. Here Lermontov's speech acquires a specifically declamatory character: loud oratorical intonation (questions and exclamations), effects of timbre, typical emphases on epithets, on emotional appositions and repetitions:

> Ликует буйный Рим..... торжественно гремит
> Рукоплесканьями широкая арена:
> А он, - пронзенный в грудь - безмолвно он лежит,
> Во прахе и крови скользят его колена...
> . . . .
> Что знатным и толпе сраженный гладиатор?
> Он презрен и забыт ...... освистанный актер.
> . . . .
> Он видит круг семьи, оставленный для брани,
> Отца, простершего немеющие длани,
> Зовущего к себе опору дряхлых дней....
> Детей играющих - возлюбленных детей.
> . . . .
> Напрасно: - жалкий раб, - он пал как зверь лесной,
> Бесчувственной толпы минутною забавой....
> . . . .
> Насмешливых льстецов несбыточные сны.

> *Tempestuous* Rome rejoices... *triumphantly* thunders
> The broad arena with applause:
> *But he - pierced through the breast - silently lies,*
> His knees slip in the dust and blood...
> . . . .
> What is a slain gladiator to the mighty and the crowd?
> He is despised and forgotten... *an actor hissed off the stage.*

120

. . . .
He sees the family circle abandoned for battle,
His father's outstretched *numbing* palms
Summoning support for his decrepit days...
Children playing - beloved children
. . . .
In vain: pathetic slave - he fell like a forest beast,
A momentary amusement for the *insensitive* crowd
. . . .
The *unrealized* dreams of *derisive* sycophants.

The sole poem of 1835 -- "Again folk orators" -- opens up this new lyric sphere in Lermontov. Though this poem usually calls to mind Pushkin's "To the Slanderers of Russia," this link should be considered as accidental or in any case uncharacteristic, because Pushkin's poem itself is not characteristic for him and did not leave any serious trace in his creative work. Rather one should recall here the names of Tyutchev, Shevyryov, Khomyakov, not to speak of their "influence" on Lermontov, but to indicate the existence of a soil on which such a poem could arise. A path to oratorical lyric poetry is broken here, which did not grow into a special genre in Lermontov because it does not develop into a special *composition* and does not become a structural whole (as in Tyutchev), but remains at the level of oratorical improvisation.

"The Mermaid" is a new attempt at a ballad on a traditional theme but, as I said above, applying a rhythmic innovation: variations of anacrusis, which link this poem to Lermontov's youthful lyric poetry. The ballad plot remains secondary, and the verse and stylistic features of the ballad form are brought to the fore. The epic genre is diminished and a lyric coloration emerges. The ballad is diminished in size and deprived of traditional plot effects: instead of a tale of a knight's death we have the song of a mermaid; instead of a dramatized narrative in which epic intonation alternates with emotional-dialogic intonation we have a smooth lyric intonation which, uncomplicated by any contrastive movements, runs to the end and concludes the ballad with a repetition of the initial stanza. The very character of verse sound is changed: instead of the declamatory euphony customary for the genuine ballad, and which is linked to the very character of its articulation (to its speech mimicry) and distinguished by an accumulation of sharply sounding, expressive consonants, we have here a much smoother euphony not so much of an articulatory-mimetic as of a musical type:[47]

Русалка плыла по реке голубой
Озаряема полной луной;

121

> И старалась она доплеснуть до луны
> Серебристую пену волны.

> The mermaid swam along the blue river
> Illumined by the full moon;
> And she tried to splash to the moon
> The silvery foam of a wave.

The basic euphonic effect here is entrusted to the sound groups which do not possess a special articulatory, enunciative expressiveness (swam, blue, full moon, splash to the moon). Apparently Heine's ballad ("Die Nixen") served as material for this ballad. In general, Lermontov begins to employ Heine's verses from this point on but selects from among them only those which suit his own tendencies ("The Pine"), or changes them to suit himself ("They loved one another").[48] "The Mermaid" is close to Heine's poem in rhythm and certain details:

> Am einsamen Strande platschert die Flut,
> Der Mond ist aufgegangen,
> Auf weisser Dune der Ritter ruht,
> Von bunten Traumen befangen.
> . . . .
> Die funfte kusst des Ritters Hand',
> Mid Sehnsucht und Verlangen;
> Die sechste zogert und kusst am End'
> Die Lippen und die Wangen.

But Heine concludes his ballad with an ironic *pointe* ("Der Ritter ist klug, es fällt ihm nicht ein, Die Augen öffnen zu müssen"), and thus parodies the traditional ballad plot, whereas Lermontov remains serious to the very end.

The third lyric poem for 1836 -- "A Branch of Palestine" -- originates in Zhukovsky's school: a melancholy meditation in the style of such poems by Zhukovsky as "To a familiar genius flown by" or "The Mysterious Visitor":[49]

> Скажи, кто ты, пленитель безымянный,
> С каких небес примчался ты ко мне?
> Зачем опять влечешь к обетованной,
> Давно, давно покинутой стране?
>
> ("К мимопролет. знак. гению")

Tell me who you are, nameless charmer,
From what heavens have you rushed to me?
Why do you again beckon to the Promised Land,
Abandoned long, long ago?

                                ("To a familiar genius...")

Both in Zhukovsky and in Lermontov the interrogative system possesses not a practical semantic, not a thematic, but an intonational significance, and it is the stylistic device which defines the entire composition. Here Lermontov is distinguished from Zhukovsky only by the introduction of the decorative ballad element into the traditional meditation; this is characteristic of his poetics. Instead of Zhukovsky's abstract lyrical meditation, we get something resembling a ballad with exotic coloration (Palestine, the Levant, the poor sons of Solim, palms, etc.) and with a hint of a plot ("The best warrior in God's host," etc.).

On the whole the lyric poetry for 1836 shows perfectly clearly that, having moved away from his youthful period, Lermontov is focusing his attention on three forms: the oratorical, declamatory "meditation," the ballad with a weakened plot, and the melancholy meditation. In the future Lermontov develops principally these three forms, altering and complicating them by introducing different stylistic variations. If poems with a folkloric coloration ("Borodino," "A Cossack Lullaby," and others) and lyrics of an album type are added here, then we get a general idea of the nature of all Lermontov's lyric poetry for the period 1836-1841.

The poem written on the death of Pushkin (1837) is a vivid example of Lermontov's oratorical style and declamatory verse line. Before us is the orator's passionate speech: successive oral periods form an entire scale of vocal timbres from a mournful to an angry note full of menace; pathetic repetitions, exclamations and questions occur in the intervals between these periods and one senses emotional gesticulation behind them:

Восстал он против мнений света
Один, как прежде.... и убит!
Убит!.... к чему теперь рыданья,
                          и т. д.

. . . .
Что ж? веселитесь! . . . .
. . . .
И что за диво? ...
. . . .
И он убит - и взят могилой
. . . .

123

Зачем поверил он словам и ласкам ложным,
Он, с юных лет постигнувший людей?..
. . . .
    А вы, надменные потомки

                    и т. д.

       He rose against the opinions of society
       Alone, as before... and he was killed!
       Killed!... what use is sobbing now
                         etc.
       . . . .
       Well? Be merry!...
       . . . .
       And what is so extraordinary?
       . . . .
       And he is killed - and taken by the grave
       . . . .
       Why did he believe false words and caresses,
         He who had understood people since youth?...
       . . . .
       And you, haughty offspring
                        etc.

As in "The Dying Gladiator" too, the oratorical intonation falls with special vigor on the epithets, owing to which they come to the fore and cluster in entire groups:

Отравлены его последние мгновенья
Коварным шопотом насмешливых невежд,
И умер он - с напрасной жаждой мщенья,
С досадой тайною обманутых надежд. 50

       His last moments were poisoned
       By the *perfidious* whisper of *derisive* ignoramuses,
       And he died - with a *vain* thirst for revenge,
       With the *secret* vexation of *deceived hopes.*

As always in Lermontov the semantic details drown in this stream of words; a phrase is turned into an uninterrupted expressive formula, into an emotional fusion. The poem operates precisely by the general force of emotional expressiveness, and not by means of semantic details and "images." The images and set phrases in themselves do not represent anything especially original or new; for the most part they are completely traditional and go back to Zhukovsky's epistle ("To Prince Vyazemsky and V. L. Pushkin"), which speaks about the death of V. A. Ozerov:[51]

Зачем он свой сплетать венец
Давал завистникам с друзьями?
Пусть дружба нежными перстами
Из лавров свой венец свила -
В них зависть терния вплела!
И торжествует! Растерзали
Их иглы славное чело -
Простым сердцам смертельно зло:
Певец угаснул от печали.
. . . .
Потомство грозное, отмщенья!

    Why did he permit the envious and their
        friends to braid his crown?
    Let friendship with tender fingers
    Weave its crown of laurel --
    Envy has woven thorns into them!
    And it triumphs! Their spines
    Have torn a glorious brow --
    Evil is fatal to simple hearts:
    The singer died of sadness.
    . . . .
    Fierce posterity, vengeance!

The proximity of Lermontov's poem to this fragment is revealed not only in the words and images (a laurel crown in which envy has woven thorns, needles, etc.), but in the movement of themes and in the construction of the verse syntax itself:

Зачем от мирных нег и дружбы простодушной
Вступил он в этот свет, завистливый и душный
    Для сердца вольного и пламенных страстей? -
Зачем он руку дал клеветникам ничтожным,
Зачем поверил он словам и ласкам ложным,
    Он, с юных лет постигнувший людей?..

И прежний сняв венок - они венец терновый,
Увитый лаврами, надели на него:
    Но иглы тайные сурово
    Язвили славное чело;
. . . .
Но есть, есть божий суд, наперсники разврата,
    Есть грозный судия: он ждет
               и т. д.

Why from peaceful comforts and simple-hearted friendship
Did he enter into that world, envious and stifling
For a free heart and ardent passions? -
Why did he give his hand to insignificant slanderers,
Why did he believe false words and caresses,
    He, who had understood people since youth?...

And removing the former garland, they placed on him
A crown of thorns entwined with laurel:
    But the concealed spines roughly
    Wounded a glorious brow;
. . . .
But there is, there is God's judgement, confidants of depravity,
    There is a menacing judge: he is waiting
                                              etc.

As we see, even in this instance Lermontov remains faithful to his method: he takes ready-made material and develops it in his own fashion, sharpening his basic, dominant element: the emotional, declamatory expressiveness of verse language.

This oratorical tendency in Lermontov is developed especially in the years
following 1837. In "A Meditation" (1838) we already have a perfectly clear
example of this style. Lermontov's penchant for forming "memorable verse
lines," formulae and maxims, found its full expression here. "A Meditation"
consists of an inter-weaving of such expressive formulae sharpened by antitheses and emotional epithets:

Богаты мы, едва из колыбели,
Ошибками отцов и поздним их умом,
И жизнь уж нас томит, как ровный путь без цели,
    Как пир на празднике чужом.
    К добру и злу постыдно равнодушны,
В начале поприща мы вянем без борьбы;
Перед опасностью позорно-малодушны,
И перед властию - презренные рабы.

Scarcely out of the cradle we are rich
With the mistakes of our fathers and their belated wisdom,
And life already torments us like a smooth, aimless road,
Like a feast at a foreign holiday.
We are shamefully indifferent to good and evil;
At the beginning of a career we fade without a struggle;
Disgracefully faint-hearted in the face of danger,
And contemptible slaves before power.

126

We find also in "A Meditation," where they are further reinforced by rhetorical and rhythmic effects, stylistic formations familiar to us from "The Dying Gladiator" and the poem on the death of Pushkin: "the momentary amusement of an insensitive crowd," "the perfidious whisper of derisive ignoramuses," "with the secret vexation of deceived hopes." These formations are not so much semantic as emotional and declamatory formulae with an emphasis upon timbre and intonation:

Мы иссушили ум наукою бесплодной,
Тая завистливо от ближних и друзей
Надежды лучшие и голос благородный
    Неверием осмеянных страстей.[52]

. . . .
И прах наш, с строгостью судьи и гражданина,
Потомок оскорбит презрительным стихом,
Насмешкой горькою обманутого сына
    Над промотавшимся отцом.

> We have desiccated the mind with sterile science,
> Enviously concealing from close ones and friends
> Our *best* hopes and a *noble* voice
> With the *disbelief* of *ridiculed* passions.
> . . . .
> And our ashes, with the severity of a judge and citizen
> A descendant will offend with *contemptuous* verse,
> With the *bitter* ridicule of a *deceived* son
> For a father who *squandered his means.*

The form noted in "The Dying Gladiator," which is structured on a comparison, is presented anew in the poem "The Poet" (1838); it is structured so that the first part develops independently as a special lyric theme, and only toward the end proves to be material for a comparision ("Are you not that way, o European world"). This is a typical oratorical device: to begin a speech with a description of some concrete fact or object and, having developed it in detail, then switch to the basic theme, thereby transforming everything that has gone before into an introductory comparison. The larger half of "The Poet" is taken up with a description of the dagger which once was taken by a "brave Cossack from a gentleman's cold corpse," and now --

Игрушкой золотой он блещет на стене,
    Увы, бесславный и безвредный!

127

It glitters on the wall like a gold toy
Alas, inglorious and harmless!

After this follows, as also was the case in "The Dying Gladiator":

В наш век изнеженный не так ли ты, поэт,
Свое утратил назначенье

и т. д.

Poet, in our effete age *did you not likewise*
Lose your calling

etc.

The very material of the comparison has, of course, a secondary meaning, and in this case as well as in many others, represents a popular cliche which became firmly established on the basis of exotic and "military" motifs in the lyric poetry contemporary to Lermontov.[53] The very fact of such a structure, such a development of the theme, has fundamental stylistic significance and reveals Lermontov's attraction to the forms of oratorical speech. It is characteristic that Belinsky was somewhat confused by the accentuated rhetoricism of this poem and reproached Lermontov for his concluding metaphor:

Проснешься ль ты опять, осмеянный пророк!
Иль никогда, на голос мщенья,
Из золотых ножен не вырвешь свой клинок,
Покрытый ржавчиной презренья?...

Will you awaken again, ridiculed prophet!
Or never, to the voice of revenge,
Will you not withdraw from its gold sheath your blade
Covered with the rust of contempt?

'"The rust of contempt' is an imprecise expression and reminds one too much of an allegory." He remarks that in Lermontov generally "a vagueness of images and inaccuracy in expression" is encountered, and contrasts Pushkin to him, in whom "one scarcely can find even a single somewhat imprecise or *recherché* expression, or even word."

A whole series of poems of 1839-1841 belongs to this type of oratorical speech-"meditations": "Do not trust yourself," "The 1st of January," "The Last Housewarming," "The Fatherland." In place of the youthful attempts to write in the English verse line of unequal syllables we see here a return to the

Alexandrine verse line (iambic hexameter), at one time so ridiculed by A. Odoevsky, a return to French eloquence. The epigraph from Barbier which Lermontov affixed to the poem "Do not trust yourself" attests to this. Lermontov's eloquence is especially and richly developed in the poem "The Last Housewarming" (1840). This is an extensive political ode written with great oratorical pathos which reminds us of Hugo's odes or some of Lamartine's meditations. The very form of the stanza (the first 3 stanzas are in the Alexandrine verse line, the fourth is shortened) is typical of French poetry:

> Меж тем как Франция, среди рукоплесканий
> И кликов радостных, встречает хладный прах
> Погибшего давно среди немых страданий
> В изгнаньи мрачном и цепях
>
> и т. д.

> Whereas France, amidst applause
> And joyful cries, greets the cold ashes
> Of the long deceased amidst mute suffering
> in gloomy exile and chains
>
> etc.

Similarly in Lamartine ("Providence for Man"- Polezhaev's translation):

> Не ты ли, о мой сын, восстал против меня?
> Не ты ли порицал мои благодеянья
> И, очи отвратя от прелести созданья,
> Проклял отраду бытия?

> Did you not, my son, arise against me?
> Did you not censure my good deeds
> And, averting your eyes from the charm of creation,
> Curse the joy of existence?

We find typical oratorical devices here, as well as in previous poems of this kind: contrasts of timbres and intonations, emotional repetitions, expressive formulae, etc. The short lines concluding each stanza are invested with special semantic and expressive force: the main *pointes* of the ode are concentrated here. Repeating the words from the end of the preceding stanza at the beginning of the next stanza likewise is characteristic of the ode's style as an oratorical form:

> Негодованию и чувству дав свободу,

129

Поняв тщеславие сих праздничных забот,
Мне хочется сказать великому народу:
    Ты жалкий и пустой народ!
Ты жалок потому, что Вера, Слава, Гений
                и т. д.

. . . .
Тогда, отяготив позорными цепями,
Героя увезли от плачущих дружин,
И на чужой Скале, за синими морями,
    Забытый, Он угас один -
Один - замучен мщением бесплодным
              и т. д.

Having granted free rein to indignation and feeling,
Having understood the vanity of these frivolous cares,
I wish to say to a great people:
    You are a *pathetic* and empty people!
You are pathetic because Faith, Glory, Genius
              etc.

. . . .
Than, having burdened him with shameful chains,
They led the hero away from the weeping detachments,
And on an alien Cliff, beyond the blue seas,
    Forgotten, he died *alone*
Alone - tormented by sterile revenge.
          etc.

The first half of the ode is set off from the second by a sharp contrast in intonation and timbre (as in the poem on the death of Pushkin)

Один, - Он был везде, холодный, неизменный,
Отец седых дружин, любимый сын молвы,
В степях египетских, у стен покорной Вены,
    В снегах пылающей Москвы!
А вы что сделали, скажите, в это время?
Когда в полях чужих Он гордо погибал,
Вы потрясали власть избранную как бремя?
    Точили в темноте кинжал?
            и т. д.

Alone, He was everywhere, cold, unchanging,
A father of grey detachments, a beloved son of rumor,
In the Egyptian steppes, at the walls of humble Vienna,
In the snows of flaming Moscow!
And what did you do, pray tell, at that time?
When in foreign fields He proudly was perishing,
Did you shake the elect power like a burden?
Did you whet a dagger in the dark?
etc.

It is interesting that even here we find the emotional, rhetorical fusion typical of Lermontov. Its semantic content has been suppressed by the general expressiveness of the idiom:

Ты жалок потому, что Вера, Слава, Гений,
Все, все великое, священное земли,
С насмешкой глупою ребяческих сомнений
Тобой растоптано в пыли.

You are pathetic because Faith, Glory, Genius,
Everything, everything great, sacred to the earth,
With the stupid mockery of childish doubts
Has been trampled by you in the dust.

On the basis of the afore-indicated examples one can assert that this is a spesial rhythmic-syntactic and intonational formula in Lermontov's oratorical style, which has its own specific form and constantly recurs: "the momentary amusement of an insensitive crowd," "the unrealized dreams of derisive sycophants," "the perfidious whisper of derisive ignoramuses," etc. The main expressive role here is entrusted to epithets; the remaining words resound weakly. If the epithets are withdrawn, then combinations of words sometimes occur which cause bewilderment: "with the ridicule of doubts." Of course, such combinations are impossible in Pushkin's language. Lermontov operates with entire word fusions, investing one of them with primary emotional stress and not troubling about the rest.[54]

4

The development of an oratorical style arose as a consequence of the decline of the intimate, lyric genres: classical romances, elegies, songs, prayers, and so on. Intimate lyric poetry had to switch to the new genres of Fet's romances, "melodies" and landscapes--to genres in which intonational emphasis had become the basic, dominating idea. Lermontov straddles these two periods. On the one hand this is manifested in his vacillations between different styles and genres; on the other hand, in his attraction to the ballad and romance lyrics with a plot.

For the period 1837-1841 one can trace a certain evolution. Basic tendencies are charted by Lermontov in the poetry of 1837. Alongside "The Death of a Poet," which is followed in the ensuing years by declamatory "meditations" and odes, we have such poems as "The Prisoner," "The Neighbor," "The Dagger," "To Kazbek." There are hints that these poems as plot pieces, as lyric tales, can be linked to a specific situation in the past or present, to the description of the setting. In the first two a "prison" motif is projected which later is repeated in such pieces as "The Neighbor Lady," "The Captive Knight." Sometimes the motif is painted in folklore tones and assumes the character of a thieves' song ("The Neighbor Lady," 1840), sometimes it changes into the monologue of a medieval knight and approximates the ballad genre ("The Captive Knight," 1840). Lermontov seemingly avoids immediate forms of lyric poetry now; he needs special accessories, a special setting or situation so that the lyric theme might acquire the character of a story. In "The Dagger" we have something on the order of a frame tale. A recollection of the past develops in connection with the apostrophe to the dagger ("I love you, my damask dagger"):

> Лилейная рука тебя мне поднесла
> В знак памяти, в минуту расставанья,
> И в первый раз не кровь вдоль по тебе текла,
> Но светлая слеза - жемчужина страданья.

> A lily-white hand proffered you to me
> As a memento, at the moment of parting,
> And for the first time not blood flowed along you
> But a bright tear - a pearl of suffering.

In the poem "To Kazbek" the lyric theme is presented as the prayer of a wanderer hurrying northward and is complicated by descriptive material which later finds itself in a new passage in the ballad "The Quarrel" (1841). There is a veiled plot even in "A Prayer"("Mother of God, with a prayer before you today") and a concrete situation is presented. This poem is notable for its rhythmic-syntactic structure; here Lermontov imparts the special character of a song to the customary dactyl, converting the first and third feet into trisyllabic anacruses so that the verse line breaks into two halves (each with 6 syllables) with one metrical stress in each half (on the fourth syllable).[55]

This rhythmic-intonational movement, which forces each phrase to split into two parts, exerts pressure on the syntax. Indeed, the phrases break down into two halves creating syntactic parallelism for the most part, but not without difficulty. We have a complete coincidence of rhythm and syntax in such lines as "Not for salvation, not before battle," "Bright youth, calm old age," "Не о спасении, не перед битвою," "Молодость светлую, старость покойную," but in the closing lines the syntax becomes more complex:

Ты восприять пошли к ложу печальному
Лучшего ангела душу прекрасную.

Send thou to the melancholy bed to receive
The beautiful soul [of?] the best angel.

Rhythmic inertia forced Lermontov to make such a word transposition as a result of which the sense of the sentence proves to be obscured "The beautiful soul" is so removed from its verb ("to receive") that "of the best angel" can be taken for the genitive case (the soul of an angel), whereas, evidently, this phrase must mean "send the best angel to receive her beautiful soul." As we noted the presence of declamatory fusions in Lermontov's oratorical verse, so we see here a rhythmic-syntactic fusion. Both attest to a destruction of the equilibrium between the verse line and the word characteristic of Lermontov's epoch.

The descriptive meditation appears in place of the old elegy. At first this meditation assumes the semblance of a strict period ("When the yellowing cornfield waves"), but in point of fact is not fully realized as it does not provide a genuine semantic gradation; rather it is an enumeration, made on the basis of a rhythmic-intonational gradation. This again is an example of a lack of convergence between verse tendencies and their verbal realization.[56] Lermontov found a new form for this kind of meditation later in the poem "I set off alone upon the road" 1841). It was the form of the romance which actually entered as romance into the repertoire of "folk" singing.

A weakening of the meditative style is noticeable in the verse of 1838 and 1839; oratorical verse comes to the fore, which I already have spoken about ("A Meditation," "The Poet," "Do Not Trust Yourself"), along with ballads ("Three Palms," "The Gifts of the Terek"). These are years of active work on prose (A Hero of Our Time) which apparently drew Lermontov away from poetry. The years 1840-1841 are again rich in verse (more than 45 pieces, while in 1838 there are about 10 in all). Here both the oratorical

("The 1st of January," "The Last Housewarming") and the balladic style ("The Aerial Ship," "Tamara," "Princess of the Sea") attain their culmination. Completing "The Novice" and "The Demon," Lermontov moves away from the narrative poem and concentrates on the ballad.[57] His tendency toward lyric poetry with a plot is realized in this form, though not linked with the construction of tales. In his hands the ballad becomes lyric narration, a "legend." For here we find a series of allegorical landscapes in which Lermontov apparently frees himself from his erstwhile favorite similes and develops his allegories without the former "thuses" in the form of special, small ballads ("The Pine," "Stormclouds," "The Cliff"). And here too is pure lyric poetry in the form of album verses and fragments ("Why," "Gratitude") with concluding *pointes*. The language of the early lyrics with its emotional intensity and the element of pathos is abandoned completely: its death sentence is pronounced in the poem "From the album of S. N. Karamzina (1840):

> Любил и я в былые годы,
> В невинности души моей,
> И бури шумные природы,
> И бури тайные страстей.
> Но красоты их безобразной
> Я скоро таинство постиг,
> И мне наскучил их несвязный
> И оглушающий язык.

> I, too, loved in bygone years,
> In the innocence of my soul,
> Both the noisy storms of nature,
> And the secret storms of passions.
> But I soon gained the secret
> Of their hideous beauty
> And became bored with their
> Incoherent and deafening language.

The end of this poem ("And Johnny Myatlev's verse") ["I Ishki Myatleva stikhi"] underscores Lermontov's break with the former lyric style. A lowering of style ensues: this is seen both in "The Fatherland" with its "Flemishness," and in the poem "It's both boring and sad" with its prose intonations and general weakening of the rhythmic movement. The very concept of a poetic genre has been liquidated here; the liberation from this concept constitutes the hidden literary historical force of this poem. This striving to go beyond the limits of genres also leads Lermontov to the free form of the epistle ("I write to you," 1840),[58] in which the tradition of Zhukovsky's descriptive epistles again comes to the fore. Finally, it should be noted that the poems

134

"A Dream" and "A Rendezvous" (1841) also are lyric tales, similarly unbounded by special generic traditions, which sum up Lermontov's attraction to lyric poetry with a plot. The first is constructed as a circular plot. The circular structure traditional for lyric forms is motivated by plot here, that of a dual dream. The return to the beginning ("And she dreamed of the valley of Daghestan") proves to be not a simple lyric ending but the actual end of a lyric tale. "The Rendezvous," which conforms perfectly to the norms of the tale, as well as the romance, is a combination characteristic of Lermontov's last years. Before us is an entire tale with a detailed description of the landscape and setting, down to the slightest details ("Your house with the smooth roof"), with an exact indication of time and place ("The evening ray died out," "Tiflis was embraced by silence"), and with a hero, a heroine, and a rival ("the young Tatar"). Moreover, the poem is written so that the time of the events themselves and the narrative time seemingly coincide. This is not a narrative about the past, but a monologue uttered during the very course of the events and the emotions, breaking off precisely at the point where the hero must begin to act rather than wait and reflect:

> Чу! близкий топот слышится.....
> А! это ты, злодей! -

> Hark! the tramp of feet is heard nearby...
> Ah! it's you, villain! --

Thus, it is possible to state that this ending is motivated on the level of plot, for clearly the rival's appearance must interrupt the tale or monologue. The very tempo of the poem gradually quickens in connection with this denouement: from the slow initial description interrupted by reflections, we pass on to the more emotionally-charged depiction of the Georgian wives leaving the baths; from here to impatience, then to suspicions which already are expressed in the form of emotional exclamations ("Your black treachery// Is clear to me, snake!"), and finally to the closing "Ah! It's you, villain!" which breaks off this furious rush of feelings. Furthermore, this poem is distinguished by a specific aiming at euphony and intonation which, probably, also furthered its penetration into the same repertoire of folk singing (mainly in a prison milieu, it seems, as in "The Neighbor Lady"). The intensified emphasis on stressed vowels and, in connection with this, their special perceptibility, is created by the very nature of the rhythm: something analogous to what occurred in the poem "I, Mother of God" happens here. The iambic trimeter with alternating dactylic and masculine rhymes acquires a particular

135

movement owing to the recurring weakening or destruction of the second metrical stress. The verse line divides into two parts, one of which is something like a dactylic foot with a monosyllabic anacrusis (∪∪—∪) and the second either repeats the very same movement or has a pause (masculine rhyme) after the stress. We get lines like: "And the guardian angels//Beneath the fresh plane tree, and with a timid step,//Here by the deserted street,//Beyond the tall poplar,//Here by the cold dampness" or "They were filled with a living fragrance,//Over sinful people,//They converse with children,//On the gloomy mountain," etc. ["И ангелы-хранители,/Под свежею чинарою,/И поступью несмелою,/Вот улицей пустынною,/За тополью высокою,/Вот сыростью холодною," or "Наполнились живым,/Над грешными людьми,/Беседуют с детьми,/На сумрачной горе," и т. д.] A variant of this basic type occurs in verse where the word-division is located not after the fourth, but after the third syllable ("But by a solitary candle,//Impatiently with a dagger,//They redden beyond the mists,//They set off with caravans"); this is felt particularly in lines with masculine rhymes: "It rushed from the East,//Along the ringing pavement,//A young Tatar,//On a Persian stallion."

"Но свечкой одинокою,/Кинжалом в нетерпении,/Краснеют за туманами,/Выходят с караванами". . . "С востока понесло,/По звонкой мостовой,/Татарин молодой,/Персидским жеребцом".] It is remarkable that the first rhythmic type predominates in the slow introductory portion of the poem, while the second type appears together with the increase in tempo. The fact is that post-tonic syllables (that is, dactylic) are pronounced with a certain lengthening, whereas pre-tonic syllables (that is, the anapestic segment) are pronounced with a certain increase in tempo and greater stress on the accent. In the given instance, apparently, we also have a corresponding rhythmic variation: from an accumulation of post-tonic to an accumulation of pre-tonic syllables. On the one hand, a special intonational cadence is created by this kind of rhythmic movement, and on the other, a special articulatory and acoustical expressiveness of vowel and consonant sounds (sonorant, fricative, and affricates).[59] Everything taken together makes this piece exceptionally important in Lermontov's creative work as a certain culminating point in his verse and genre tendencies. Incidentally, I shall mention that also in the poem "I set off alone upon the road" the trochaic pentameter meter undergoes just such a rhythmic alteration as a result of which each verse line falls into two parts: one quicker with anacrustic syllables (∪∪—), the other slower with various types of word divisions. In this fashion the trochaic pentameter acquires a unique character and changes the intonation into a melody.[60]

Thus, in the verse of his last years Lermontov chiefly consolidated the forms of oratorical and romance lyrics with a plot; from these forms on the one hand, the way leads further to Nekrasov, and on the other to Ap. Grigorev, Polonsky, Ogarev, and, to a certain degree, Fet.[61]

It remains for me to speak about Lermontov's folkloric verse and his comic narrative poems. In the youthful period his interest in folklore is linked chiefly to rhythmic experiments and a general attraction to the romance style. Along with his departure from metrical innovations the attraction to folklore died out, for from 1832 until 1837 there are no experiments in this style. In 1837 "Borodino" and "The Song about Tsar Ivan Vasilevich" appear, and in 1840 "A Cossack Lullaby" and "The Neighbor Lady." These pieces are symptomatic for the history of Russian poetry as an index of a cooling toward purely literary, lyric poetry; it is not accidental that Koltsov's appearance met with such enthusiasm in literary circles. In Lermontov's creative activity these pieces coincide with a period of cooling toward the traditional narrative poem. "The Song about Tsar Ivan Vasilevich" is an experiment in the use of the historical song for constructing a Russian narrative poem. Apparently its appearance is connected with Lermontov's disappointment in "The Boyar Orsha," a piece which also was supposed to have represented a historical poem but which could not satisfy Lermontov, since its national and historical material proved to be simply affixed to the traditional Byronic poem. Thus, rather than any serious and path-breaking event, in Lermontov's creative activity, too, this "Song" is a symptom characteristic of his evolution; on the one hand it confirms Lermontov's inclination toward plot forms and, on the other hand, his disappointment with his youthful verse. In his remaining pieces Lermontov employs the material of military and thieves' folklore, changing it into the form of a plotted romance or ballad. In general this sally into folklore demonstrates a striving to strengthen the projected genres with national material, a striving which arose naturally to displace the fascination with Western poetry.

In a period of the formation of a pathetic style a counter tendency usually arises toward comic style, satire and parody (Byron, Musset, Hoffman, Gogol). Artistic devices per se lie outside these categories; an impression of the tragic or the comic is produced due to one or another psychological motivations which require a specific perception. Precisely for this reason it is one step from the tragic to the comic, and precisely for this reason the most intense pathos provides the best material for parody. By taking conventional forms, and thereby losing motivation, the high pathetic element easily switches to the comic; all that is necessary is to violate slightly the unity of lexical material or the unity of intonation. It seems that none of the Russian poets has been parodied so readily as Lermontov, and this is wholly under-

137

standable. But Lermontov himself time and again turned to the comic style and even to self-parody. His first experiments in this sphere date from as far back as 1830 with "The Boulevard" and "Asmodey's Feast." A notation dates from this year: "Curse everyone in the next satire and only one sad stanza. Say just before the end that I have written in vain, and that should this pen turn into a stick, and some modern divinity strike them -- all the better." In 1831 there is another project: "Write a playful narrative poem 'The Adventures of a Bogatyr'." A project to which Lermontov returned in 1838 ("A Fairytale for Children") dates from this same year: "Write a long satirical poem 'The Adventures of a Demon'." As should be expected *a priori*, the plot of "The Demon" immediately presents itself in Lermontov's mind on two planes: the pathetic and the comic, as a lyrico-epic poem ("tale") and as a satire. This probably explains such breaks in the pathetic style as the line "And it should be said - it's about time!" from an 1833 draft (see above). It likewise is to be expected that Lermontov would turn to the narrative poem in the style of Byron's "Beppo" or Musset's "Namouna," where lyrical and comic stanzas will alternate and where the plot itself will occasion constant digressions from it and a play with motivation. Indeed, in "Sashka" we have this kind of poem, which, on the one hand, incorporates material from the youthful lyrico-narrative poems and from the lyric poetry, and on the other, from the "Junker" narrative poems. The poem's first stanza announces a departure from the former pathetic style:

> Наш век смешон и жалок: все пиши
> Ему про казни, цепи да изгнанья,
> Про темные волнения души,
> И только слышишь муки да страданья.
> . . . .
> Впадал я прежде в эту слабость сам
> И видел от нее лишь вред глазам;
> Но нынче я не тот уж, как бывало, -
> Пою, смеюсь. - Герой мой добрый малый.

> Our age is ludicrous and pathetic: all it cares about
> Is executions, chains and exile,
> About dark anxieties of the soul,
> And one hears only torments and sufferings,
> . . . .
> I myself formerly fell into this weakness
> And saw in it only harm to my eyes;
> But nowadays I'm not at all the same as then, --

I sing, I laugh - my hero is a kind lad.

A play on digressions occurs already in stanza V:

Будь терпелив, читатель милый мой!
Кто б ни был ты: внук Евы иль Адама,
Разумник ли, шалун ли молодой, -
Картина будет; это - только рама!
От правил, утвержденных стариной,
Не отступлю -

> Be patient, my dear reader!
> Whoever you may be: the grandson of Eve or Adam,
> A clever, or young mischievous fellow, --
> There will be a picture; this is only the frame!
> From rules codified in olden times
> I will not deviate --

and thereby emphasizes a departure from "the rules." In place of a narrative about the hero there are lines about Moscow and Napoleon,[62] and, later, irony at the expense of the muse and parody of his own comparisons:

Луна катится в зимних облаках,
Как щит варяжский или сыр голландской.
Сравненье дерзко, но люблю я страх
Все дерзости, по вольности дворянской.

> The moon rolls along in the wintry clouds
> Like a Varangian shield, or a Dutch cheese.
> The simile is bold, but I love terribly
> All boldnesses, as befits aristocratic license.

Further in this same vein: "And chandeliers were reflected in the mirrors, Like stars in a puddle." Serious elegiac stanzas and ordinary comparisons turn up alongside this material; it is all material which Lermontov uses later in such works as "To the Memory of A. I. Odoevsky" (see above) or "The lst of January".[63] The play with motivation is bared especially where it is necessary to switch to the tale about the past (stanza XLIX):

Роман, вперед!... Не идет? - Ну, так он
Пойдет назад. Герой наш спит покуда,
Хочу я рассказать, кто он, откуда,
Кто мать его была, и кто отец,

139

Как он на свет родился, наконец
Как он попал в позорную обитель,
Кто был его лакей и кто учитель.

> Forward, novel!... It won't go? - Well then it
> Will go backward. While our hero sleeps
> I wish to relate, who he is and whence,
> Who was his mother and who the father,
> How he came into the world, finally
> How he came to this infamous place,
> Who was his servant and who a teacher.

A biography of his parents and Sashka himself proceeds, interrupted by discourses, comic comparisons and remarks in parentheses, which for the most part cause a break-down in the lyric or pathetic style and serve as self-parody:

О, если б мог он, как бесплодный дух,
В вечерний час сливаться с облаками,
Склонять к волнам кипучим жадный слух
И долго упиваться их речами,
И обнимать их перси, как супруг!
В глуши степей дышать со всей природой
Одним дыханьем, жить ее свободой!
О, если б мог он, в молнию одет,
Одним ударом весь разрушить свет!..
(Но к счастию для вас, читатель милый,
Он не был одарен подобной силой.)
(Строфа LXXIII)

> O, if he could, like an incorporeal spirit,
> Merge with the clouds at the evening hour,
> Incline a greedy ear to the boiling waves
> And long revel in their speeches,
> *And embrace their breasts like a spouse!*
> In a remote corner of the steppes breathe with all nature
> With one breath, live with her freedom!
> O, if he could, girded in lightning,
> Destroy the entire world with one blow!...
> *(But fortunately for you, dear reader,*
> *He was not gifted with such power.)*
> (Stanza LXXIII)

A return to the interrupted plot is accomplished by means of such play:

Теперь героев разбудить пора,
Пора привесть в порядок их одежды...

(Строфа CXXI)

Now it is time to awaken the heroes
Time to straighten up their clothes...

(Stanza CXXI.)

Tirza's late awakening is motivated by the fact that the author has been relating for a long time:

Резвый бег пера
Я не могу удерживать серьезно,
И потому она проснулась поздно...

The frisky flight of the pen
I cannot seriously restrain
And for that reason she awakened late...

The first part concludes with an entire chain of lyric stanzas which gradually changes into a satiric tone and closes with a joke:

Я кончил...Так! дописана страница.
Лампада гаснет...[64] Есть всему граница -
Наполеонам, бурям и войнам,
Тем более терпенью и ... стихам,
Которые давно уж не звучали
И вдруг с пера, бог знает как, упали!..

I have finished I... So!, the page is written.
The lamp fades out... There is a limit to everything −
To Napoleons, storms, and wars,
All the more to forbearance and... to verses,
Which for a long time have not resounded
And suddenly from the pen, God knows how, they fell!..

This recalls the last stanza of Byron's "Beppo":

My pen is at the bottom of a page,
    Which being finish'd, here the story ends;
T'is to be wish'd it had been sooner done,
But stories somehow lengthen when begun.

The link with "Beppo" shows through in various passages in "Sashka,"

141

not to mention the general style. Lermontov says in the description of Tirza:

> И с этих пор, чтоб избежать ошибки,
> Она дарила всем свои улыбки...
> (Строфа XVIII)

> And since then, to avoid a mistake,
> She favored everyone with her smiles...
> (Stanza XVIII.)

In Byron's description of Lora (stanza 23):

> Indeed she schone (sic) all smiles, and seem's to flatter
> Mankind with her black eyes for looking at her.

Lermontov says concerning Sashka's fascination with one of the servant girls (stanza XC):

> И мудрено ль? Четырнадцати лет
> Я сам страдал от каждой женской рожи.

> Is it any wonder? At fourteen years
> I myself suffered from every female mug,

In Byron (stanza 14):

> One of those forms which flit by us, when we
> Are young, and fix our eyes on every face.

Lermontov's poem remained unfinished; chapter II was only begun. But in their very essence poems of this type do not require a special ending because their basic meaning is not in the story but in the play with narrative form. In Musset's poem "Namouna" (1832), despite the presence of three "songs," nothing manages to happen; the hero, who has just emerged from the bath, remains naked while the author prepares to relate something about him. In the second song the author himself observes that he still has not related anything:

> Mon premier chant est fait. -- Je viens de le relire:
> J'ai bien mal expliqué ce que je voulais dire;
> Je n'ai plus dit un mot de ce que j'aurais dit

142

Si j'avais fait un plan une heure avant d'écrire.

The third part begins with a new acknowledgement that the plot remains untold and, in order to correct this matter, the author quickly relates the outline of what he planned to set forth in the poem:

> Puisqu'en son temps et lieu je n'ai pas pu l'écrire,
> Je vais la raconter; l'écrira qui voudra.

Lermontov's second comic poem or "fairytale" (as he himself called it), "The Paymaster's Wife" (1837), is also written like an intentional digression from the serious style, from the lyric narrative poem, as a parody. A simple anecdote from the life of the Uhlans in Tambov is turned into an entire tale with detailed descriptions of everyday life, external appearances, a characterization of the hero, etc. In the most intriguing passage, when coronet Garin arrives at the paymaster's ball, the author breaks off the tale ("But there is no need for us to hurry here") and presents two lyrical stanzas ("I hastened to live in bygone years") in which, parodying the high style, he compares himself to a young eagle in a cage:

> Глядя на горы и на дол,
> Напрасно не подъемлет крылья,
> Кровавой пищи не клюет,
> Сидит, молчит и смерти ждет.
> . . . .
> Не все ж томиться бесполезно
> Орлу за клеткою железной:
> Он свой воздушный прежний путь
> Еще найдет когда-нибудь,
> Туда, где снегом и туманом
> Одеты темные скалы,
> Где гнезда вьют одни орлы,
> Где тучи бродят караваном.

> > Looking at the mountains and the valley,
> > He does not vainly lift his wings --
> > The bloody food he does not peck
> > He sits, silent, awaiting death.
> > . . . .
> > The eagle will not always languish uselessly
> > Behind the iron cage:

143

He his former aerial way
Again will find some day,
There where in snow and fog
Dark cliffs are clothed,
Where only eagles weave nests,
Where clouds wander like a caravan.

It is remarkable that these lines later turned up in "The Novice":

Она мечты мои звала
От келий душных и молитв
В тот чудный мир тревог и битв,
Где в тучах прячутся скалы,
Где люди вольны, как орлы.

She summoned my dreams
From stifling cells and prayers
To that wonderful world of anxieties and battles
Where cliffs hide themselves in clouds,
Where people are free as eagles.

Once more this confirms that the difference between the comic and the pathetic lies not in the devices themselves nor in the material, but in the ambient motivation in the psychological commentary.

A departure from the canonical narrative poem once more is underscored by the conclusion of "The Paymaster's Wife":

И вот конец печальной были,
Иль сказки - выражусь прямей.
Признайтесь, вы меня бранили?
Вы ждали действия, страстей?
Повсюду нынче ищут драмы,
Все просят крови, даже дамы.

And here is the end of my sad but true tale,
Or fairytale - I'll express myself more directly.
Confess, you have cursed me?
You expected action, passions?
Nowadays they search for drama everywhere,
Everyone begs for blood, even ladies.

However, neither of Lermontov's poems were a novelty after Pushkin's "Count Nulin" and "The House in Kolomna." On the contrary, this was already the culmination of the comic narrative poem: from Lermontov this genre passes to Turgenev ("Parasha," "The Landowner," "Andrey") and temporarily concludes its literary existence here.

"A Fairytale for Children" (1839) is of special interest in the history of Lermontov's creative activity; in its own way it is a parody on "The Demon," which Lermontov himself speaks about

> Я прежде пел про демона инова:
> То был безумный, страстный, детский бред...
> . . . .
> Но этот чорт совсем иного сорта:
> Аристократ и не похож на чорта.

> Formerly I sang about a different demon:
> It was a mad, passionate, child's delirium...
> . . . .
> But this devil is wholly of another sort:
> An aristocrat and not at all like a devil.

Lermontov returns to his early intention: "To write a long satirical poem 'The Adventures of a Demon'." It confirms the fact that the image of the Demon has a dual function in Lermontov, as was the case in certain fragments indicated above, which were transferred from "Sashka" into "To the Memory of A. I. Odoevsky," from "The Paymaster's Wife" into "The Novice." Even certain situations and expressions from "The Demon" recur in "A Fairytale for Children." Here he is a "cunning demon," who has stolen into a girl's bedroom:

> И речь его коварных искушений
> Была полна - ведь он недаром гений!

> And his speech of perfidious temptations
> Was full - after all he was not a genius for nothing!

Leaning over the head of the bed, he speaks:

> Не знаешь ты, кто я - но уж давно
> Читаю я в душе твоей; незримо,
> Неслышно говорю с тобою - но
> и т. д.

145

> You don't know who I am - but for a long time
> I have been reading in your soul; invisibly,
> Inaudibly I have spoken with you - but
> etc.

Hinting precisely at his tragic brother, the new demon hastens to calm the girl:

> Ты с ужасом отвергнула б мою
> Безумную любовь. - Но я люблю
> По своему... терпеть и ждать могу я,
> Не надо мне ни ласк, ни поцелуя.

> With horror you would reject my
> Insane love. - But I love
> In my own way... I can endure and wait,
> I need neither caresses nor a kiss.

The tale of the demon follows, which represents the beginning of some long tale, and then the poem suddenly breaks off. One must conclude that the new fascination with prose, which had begun at that time, once and for all drew Lermontov away from "tales in verse." Having completed the reworking of his youthful narrative poems ("The Novice" and "The Demon"), Lermontov abandons the lyrical verse genres (meditations and odes, ballads and romances) and switches from the narrative poem to the novel in prose.

CHAPTER III: PROSE

1

The appearance of prose in Lermontov is linked to his disappointment in the narrative poems and dramas to which he had devoted so much effort in the years 1829-1831. The haste with which he switches from one poem to another, each time assimilating the preceding work into his new experiment, itself attests both to his constant dissatisfaction and his insistent desire to achieve some sort of result. In 1831 Lermontov vacillates between verse and prose; he thinks that it would be better to write "The Demon" in prose. This project remains unfulfilled, but then in 1832 he begins writing a novel (Vadim). This brings the problem of plot and narrative construction to the fore, a problem which plays a secondary role in the narrative poem, since the verse form itself weakens the structural significance of these elements. Plot in verse is veiled by the influence of the poetic word, by its own dynamics, with respect to which plot is only a background element. "I am writing not a novel but a novel in verse -- there is a devilish difference!" (Pushkin). *Evgeny Onegin* would have demanded much more complex motivation in prose, a much greater number of events and characters, and would not have afforded the opportunity to introduce an entire album of lyric poetry into the narration.

It is natural that Lermontov employs previous skills in his first attempt at a novel; the result is something like a narrative poem in prose. The style of "Vadim" is linked closely to the style of the youthful narrative poems and bears the imprint of verse devices. We have before us a hybrid form of "poetic prose" which, in Shevyryov's words (who contrasted it to Pushkin's prose), "borrows metaphors and similes from verse" and represents "some intermediary form between poety and prose" (*Moskvitianin,* 1841, V. No.9, p.260).By the beginning of the 30s a difference has developed between two types of prose, one of which sets itself off against the verse line and is based on the principle of contrast to poetic language; the second type, on the contrary, is oriented toward the verse line and employs all the devices of rhythmic and emotionally-elevated language. Just as in France the Chateaubriand-Hugo line stood in opposition to the Merimée-Stendhal line, among us Pushkin's prose is opposed to the prose of Marlinsky and Gogol (not to mention such writers as Mashkov, Timofeev, and others), which in part goes back to Karamzin's prose. Marlinsky, of course, cannot be confined to the concept of "poetic" or "rhetorical" prose in the total corpus of his work; such an oversimplified notion of him had already formed by the time the initial period of the organization of the literary language and narrative forms had passed. But it is important to bear in mind here the existence of a tendency toward this kind of prose itself. Lermontov is affiliated precisely with this "poetic" tendency in "Vadim."

It is impossible to call this a historical novel in the strict sense of the word; there are no historical personages or historical events proper in it. However, its action is connected with the Pugachyov rebellion, and the main hero acts against the background of impending events. This results in a peculiar combination of a narrative poem with a historical novel, a blending of genres and styles characteristic for Lermontov. Despite the historical and every-day details, Vadim remains the hero of a narrative poem; he utters eloquent monologues and has no organic link to the 18th century. Zagoskin is combined with Marlinsky here, Walter Scott and Cooper with Hugo. There is no pure narrative; it is replaced by an emotional, rhetorical commentary in the style of narrative poems. Individual formulations clearly reveal their origin. It is said about Olga that: "This was an angel driven from paradise for grieving too much about humanity." About Vadim: "Vadim possessed an unfortunate soul over which a single thought sometimes could gain unlimited power." This is from "The Lithuanian Woman:"

> В печальном только сердце может страсть
> Иметь неограниченную власть.

> Only in a sad heart can passion
> Possess unlimited power.

Yury speaks to Olga in words familiar from Lermontov's lyric poetry: "What is the world without you... a temple without a divinity..." Relating his life in the monastery (a motif linking "Vadim" to "A Confession") Vadim says: "I have spent my best years within the cloister's walls, within the stifling walls, deafened by the ringing of bells, by the singing of people dressed in black dresses, thereby thinking themselves closer to heaven." In the very same "The Lithuanian Woman" we read:

> В монастыре, далеко от людей
> (И потому не ближе к небесам).

> In a monastery far from people
> (And therefore no closer to heaven).

The rhetorical formulae and numerous similes, which for the most part conclude chapters or separate parts of chapters, likewise attest to a link with the narrative poem. Here is a characteristic ending (chapter II): "Hueless jagged walls, towers, and a church were silhouetted against the twilight horizon like flat, black cities; but there was something majestic in that spectacle which forced the soul to become absorbed in itself and to think about eternity, to think about the grandeur of the earth and heaven. Gloomy and marvelous thoughts are born at such a time, like a solitary monastery -- an immobile monument to the weakness of certain people who did not understand that where virtue is concealed, there also crime can be concealed." Yury's spiritual condition after Zara's faithlessness (the inserted story of Yury's love for Zara) is described by means of an entire series of complex comparisons: "But what did he have left from all of this? -- memories? -- yes, but what kind of memories? Bitter, deceptive memories, like fruit growing on the shores of the Dead Sea whose glistening rosy skins conceal ashes, dry hot ashes![65] And now every time at the thought of Olga Yury's heart flared up with effort and pain, like a crackling torch sprinkled with water; unevenly, fitfully it pulsed in his breast, like a lamb under the knife of a sacrifice-bearer." The lyrical digression dedicated to a girl killed by Cossacks closes with a traditional simile familiar to us from the verse: "Threatening faces surrounded your damp deathbed, a curse was your funeral oration! What a future! What a past! and everything was shattered in an instant. Thus in the evening sometimes smoky, crimson and lilac clouds gather in a crowd in the West, merge into fiery pillars and weave fantastic round dances. And a castle with towers and crenelations, marvelous as a poet's dream, grows against the blue expanse... but a northern wind blew and the clouds scattered and fell to the insensate earth as dew."

A kinship with the narrative poem's style likewise is revealed in the special kind of narrative questions which serve as a transition from some characters to others, or from one event to another: "Who is going to meet her? It's Vadim... Where was Olga? In a dark corner of her room she was lying on a trunk... Where had Vadim taken cover this entire evening? In a dark attic stretched out on the straw face up, with folded arms, he was borne away in thought into eternity... But what had Vadim been doing? O, Vadim did not like idleness!" etc. We get the same in "Izmail-Bey":

> Где ж Росламбек, кумир народа?
> Где тот, кем славится свобода? -
> Один забыт, перед огнем,
> Поодаль с пасмурным челом,
> Стоял он, жертва злой досады.

149

Where was Roslambek, the idol of the people?
Where was he, of whom freedom boasts?-
Alone, forgotten, before the fire,
At some distance with a sullen brow,
He stood, a victim of evil spite.

The same can be found in Marlinsky's prose: "But who is there leaping over the tombs drawing lightning from them? It is Osman. His white steed races along like a saddled whirlwind, and a striped cloak (*čuxa*) billows in the gloom like a cloud!" ("The Red Cloak [*pokryvalo*]). Often a character's feelings and thoughts are presented in the third-person but preserve the lyrical form, the narrator blends with his character: "Yesterday he revealed himself to Olga; finally he had found her, he had met his sister whom he had left in the cradle, finally!... O! wonderful is Nature... is it far from the brother to the sister? Ah, but what a difference! These angelic features, this demonic appearance... However, did not the angel and the demon spring from the same source?" etc.

A poetics of the deformed, the fearful - everything which so irritated Pushkin in the French "frenetic" literature of the 30's - lies at the basis of the novel. Yury Palitsyn, who would be the main hero in a novel of a different style, is moved off to the side and reduced in importance; force is preferred to nobility, even if it is united with cruelty and "villainy." Lermontov himself underscores this: "I would have wished to present Yury as a true hero, but what am I to do if he were such as you and I... there are no words against the truth. I have already said previously that only in Olga's eyes did he assume a frenzied flame, stormy desires, a proud will, and that outside this charmed circle he was a man like any other: simply a kind, intelligent youth. What's to be done!..." Vadim is made the real hero, a paradoxical villain inspiring horror by his acts as well as his deformed appearance. It is here that the kinship of "Vadim" and the "frightful" novels is revealed. Lermontov dwells at great length on the representation of horrifying or repellent scenes, describing them in minute detail; whereas in other instances he avoids detailed descriptions, declaring that "such things are not described" (Yury's meeting with his parents), or that their description "requires the talent of a Walter Scott and the patience of his readers." Reflecting in chapter VI about Olga and his future vengeance, Vadim notices two moths circling over a violet bluebell and vying with one another: "finally the multi-colored moth remained the victor; it alighted and concealed itself among the petals; vainly the other moth circled over him... he was forced to leave. Vadim had a twig in his hand; he struck the flower and killed the successful insect... and observed its last quivering with a certain delight!..." We have here the symbolic prototype of

Vadim's future struggle with Yury for possession of Olga. The comparison of Vadim to a vampire is likewise characteristic. It is a detail dating from a pseudo - Byronic tale published in 1828 in Russian:[66] in answer to Olga's question about the terrible punishment which he has prepared for Palitsyn, Vadim "burst out laughing wildly and, attempting to stop himself, bit his lower lip so firmly that blood began to flow; at that instant he resembled a vampire looking at its dying victim."

The attraction to specific effects of this kind induces Lermontov to describe minutely the scene between Vadim and the old beggar woman whose appearance horrified him: "he turned around and a loathsome spectacle arose before his eyes: a short, dried-up old woman with a large paunch, so to say, hung over him; her rolled-up sleeves bared two rake-like arms, and a bluish sarafan made up of a thousand vile rags hung crookedly and askew on that walking skeleton; the expression of her face struck one's mind with some sort of indescribable baseness, some sort of putrefaction peculiar to corpses long exposed to the air; the snub nose, the enormous mouth from which burst a sharp and strange voice, still did not mean anything in comparison with the beggarwoman's eyes! Imagine two gray circles dancing in narrow slits surrounded by red borders; neither lashes nor brows!... - and, moreover, a gaze drawing on the surface of the soul, causing a morbid constraint in all the senses!..."

A special system of "Rembrandtian" illumination[67] (contrasts of bright light and shadow) runs through the entire novel, imparting a gloomy, fantastic character to the scenes described; this pictorial element also links Lermontov's novel with the novel of horrors (including here also Hugo). There is no ordinary daylight in "Vadim": "A tallow candle burning on the table lit up her innocent, open brow and one cheek on which, if one were to look intently, could be discerned a slight golden fluff; the remainder of her face was concealed by a dense shadow... Vadim's brow darkened, and a bitter, caustic smile imparted something demonic to his features, which were weakly illuminated by the guttering candle... A strip of bright light stole into the room and fell on the lips distorted by the terrible, insulting smile; darkness covered everything all around... through the smoke of the incense the enormous chandeliers hanging in the middle of the church cast mysterious rays on the glittering fretwork and icon framework covered with pearls; the rear portion of the temple was in deep darkness" etc.

The very same exists, for example, in Maturin's *Melmoth The Wanderer*: "it was late, and the icon-lamps burned dully in the church; when he stopped at the side-altar, he stood such that the light of an icon-lamp descending from above fell only on his face and one of his arms, which he stretched out in my direction. The rest of his figure was wrapped in a darkness which lent something truly terrifying to this spectral, disembodied head" [Eikhenbaum is quoting the Russian translation here -- tr.]. The aesthetic function of this descriptive detail is especially clear in one passage in "Vadim" (chapter XV): "Around the brilliant fire kindled directly opposite the monastery gate the beggars shouted and sported more than anyone else and their joy was a frenzy; lit up by the quivering scarlet reflections of the fire, they made up the foreground of the picture; behind them everything was darker and more indistinct; people moved like sharp, crude shadows; it seemed that an unknown painter had prescribed a respectable place to these beggars, to these disgusting rags; it appeared that he exposed them to the light as the main idea, the main feature of the character of his picture."[68] The description is transferred from the realistic every-day to the metaphysical plane and transformed into a gloomy, fantastic picture.

"Vadim" remained unfinished. The problem of genre and narration remained unresolved. Lermontov was not equal to his conception of a large form; as one might have expected , the hero's declamation came to the fore and suppressed the natural movement of the plot. We have before us a struggle of genres and styles, a struggle of the narrative poem with the novel. An attempt was made to unite the style of the lyrical monologue with a narrative style, but the former clearly prevailed over the latter. Vadim, Yury and Olga repeated the group of characters customary for Lermontov's youthful narrative poems; the everyday and historical material remained weakly established and unfused into the form.

Lermontov takes up prose for the second time only after 1835, after a new attempt to return to an old draft of a lyrical poem ("A Confession") and to turn it into a historical poem ("The Boyar Orsha"). By this time a turn to prose already had appeared clearly in Russian literature; the narrative poem had become the subject of ridicule and parodies, interest in verse had begun to weaken noticeably. In place of the previous complaints about the poverty of prose, about "the absence of human life on this side" (Marlinsky), complaints of an opposite character appear: about the inordinate abundance of novels and tales. Marlinsky begins his 1833 article ("On the Novel of N. Polevoy") with the words: "It seems that F. V. Bulgarin in good time blessed us with his novels. Along the path blazed by his 'The Pretender" raced dozens of writers as if they were competing in a horse race... Moscow and Petersburg went at it head to head. A cross-fire began to blaze from all the book shops, and novel after novel flew against the head of the good Russian people." In his 1823 survey Marlinsky still cannot name any prose writers besides Karamzin, Zhukovsky, and Batyushkov. After 1828 Russian prose begins to develop quickly; by the middle of the 30s we already have a long list of authors: without mentioning Pushkin and Gogol, we have before us Bulgarin, Marlinsky, Senkovsky, Pogorelsky, Zagoskin, Odoevsky, Dal, Veltman, Grech, Kalashnikov, Lazhechnikov, Polevoy, Masalsky, Begichev, Stepanov, Voskresensky, Mashkov, etc.

2

The basic problem of this period in Russian prose is the organization of the literary language itself and a narrative form. The question of prose language is a matter of equal concern to Pushkin, Marlinsky, Odoevsky, Dal, Senkovsky, and Veltman. A struggle to revitalize the bookish language, which had frozen in the old traditions, unites them all; they would accomplish this through the infusion of elements of conversational and popular speech, or the creation of new words and phrases.

Dal immerses himself in folklore and writes his fairytales, thereby motivating the introduction of popular language into literature: "Not fairytales in themselves (he writes about himself in 1842) were important to him, but the Russian word which is so suppressed among us that it has been impossible for it to show itself in the world without a special pretext and occasion, - and the fairytale served as a pretext." This course did not satisfy Pushkin,[69] although he too sympathized with Dal's aspirations: "A fairytale is a fairytale (he said to Dal in 1832), but our language exists in its own right, and nowhere is it possible to give it this Russian expansiveness as in the fairytale... One ought to be able to learn to speak Russian even outside a fairytale... But no, it is difficult, it is still impossible!"[70]

Odoevsky also posed this problem to himself; while very interested in popular speech and, especially, noting down characteristic dialogues, at the same time he objects to the simple transference of the peculiarities of popular language into literary works even if they are representing simple folk: "This language, though crude, is powerful and picturesque; but it is still impossible to employ it; the public still is not mature enough for it."[71] In the same article Odoevsky says bluntly that it is especially difficult for the Russian writer to write novels "on the manners of the highest and lowest societies" because it is difficult for him to cope with the language of both strata: one must "find that language which would correspond both to the character of simple folk and the demands of art." Addressing his readers in "Princess Mimi," Odoevsky declares: "Do you know, kind sirs, readers, that the writing of books is a very difficult matter? That the most difficult of books for the writer are novels and tales? That the most difficult novels are those which must be written in the Russian language? That the most difficult novels in Russian are those in which the manners of present-day society are described?" In conclusion he requests his readers not to reproach him "if, for some, my heroes' conversation will seem too bookish, and for others not sufficiently grammatical. In the latter instance I refer to Griboedov, perhaps the only one who has grasped the secret of transferring our conversational language to paper."[72]

In the article on *Mirgorod* cited above, Odoevsky thinks that only Gogol succeeded in overcoming these difficulties. Apparently, here it is a matter of Gogol's literary language being constructed on a combination of Russian and Ukrainian, which preserved the unity of its lexical composition and did not break down so sharply into bookish and popular speech as did Russian. It is not by accident that at that time "Little Russia" became a constant literary theme (Kulzhinsky, Pogorelsky, Grebenka, etc.) rivaling the literary Caucasus. The fascination with the Ukrainian language, Ukrainian fairytales, etc., is bound up with the need to vivify the Russian literary language with various dialects. The use of Ukrainian granted an opportunity to lower the Russian literary style without at the same time coarsening it.

The problem of the lowering of style and the emancipation from bookish traditions was posed by everyone, but it was solved in different fashion. Some turned to folklore, to dialects, to old Russian literature ("The Igor Tale"); others began to transform the Russian literary language, employing the forms of literary speech or creating new turns of speech on the model of foreign languages (primarily French).

Marlinsky praises his own "historical tales" because in them he "cast off the fetters of the bookish language and began to speak in the living Russian idiom." Senkovsky rebelled against the traditional "Slavonicizing" and wrote in defense of his lively feuilleton language: "Instead of the too familiar Russian language, which loves to express itself in quick, short sentences, linking them with a strict, logical sequence of thought and not diverse conjunctions, you see a doleful chain of pale thoughts bound by old shackles: they slowly drag themselves along to penal servitude, to Nerchinsk, in accord with the verdict of the German period!... whoever cannot *parse* a sentence is not able to compose a Russian period and cannot write."[73]

Senkovsky's statement that the writers' styles age quickly in the unnatural situation of the Russian language at that time is very interesting: "not a quarter of a century passes and no longer can anyone read you... Lomonosov, Fonvizin, Derzhavin, Ozerov, Pushkin - why these are completely different dialects of the Russian language! Ozerov and Pushkin were (and who would have thought it) contemporaries!... A poet, a writer must take the simple, ordinary words and forms which are used in the living language and use them exclusively... For the poet and writer in particular, this pure, homogeneous element is the living language of the people to which they belong, language in that form in which it exists in nature, in the mouths of an entire nation."[74]

Senkovsky does not consider Pushkin's prose an advanced phenomenon: "What Pushkin did for poetry sooner or later would have occurred in prose, in which, as if he were not in his own element, he preserved the prejudices of his teachers; what is occurring nowadays in the language is only the consequence of and an unavoidable supplement to the Pushkinian reform in poetry." And, indeed, Pushkin's prose is remarkable as a model of mastery in plot construction, but there is no resolution in it of those stylistic problems which the prose of the 30s posed. The "simplicity" of Pushkin's prose is artificial; it is constructed on a rejection of those experiments which history demanded and without which Russian prose could not have developed. Next lay a problem not so much of the simplification of style as of its enrichment, its vivification. This was a moment when it was necessary to sacrifice both "aesthetic measure" and "taste." Acknowledging the weak development of a Russian narrative style, at the same time Pushkin did not want to "bend" it as had Marlinsky, who, in Shevyryov's words, "wanted to force images and the language." The epistolary-business style, uncomplicated by any new formations, by any rhetoric or declamation, seemed to him the sole suitable style for prose; everything else appeared affected and mannered to him ("write with all the freedom of a conversation or a letter"). Praising N. Pavlov for a "pure and free" style, he nevertheless finds a certain "affectation in his descriptions, the myopic pettiness of present-day French novelists." He prefers to confine prose within the limits of the modest novella-anecdote in which descriptions are reduced to a minimum, lyrical or philosophical digressions are absent, and nowhere does the narrator come to the fore.

Vyazemsky very faithfully described the character of Pushkin's prose (the article "A View of Our Literature in the Decade after the Death of Pushkin," 1847): "The story is always lively but deliberate and composed, perhaps too composed. It seems as if Pushkin guards himself; it is as if he strove through imposed sobriety to deflect from himself the slightest suspicion of using poetic spirits."[75] In contrast to Pushkin, Marlinsky experiments uninterruptedly, risking lapsing into mannerism, affectation, and prolixity: "I want and find a Russian language ready for anything and capable of expressing everything (he writes to his brothers). If this is my fault, it is also my merit. I am convinced that prior to me no one has given so much variety to Russian phrases."

Thus, the 30s are a period of the intense working-out of the Russian literary language. Marlinsky, Dal, Veltman, and Senkovsky must be acknowl-

155

edged as the main figures in this area; the Russian language had to be "bent" as they "bent" it, so that the prose of Gogol, Lermontov, Turgenev, Tolstoy, Leskov, and Dostoevsky could be worked out. Such writers as Odoevsky and Pavlov occupy a middle position, and Pushkin sums up the old struggle between Karamzin and the archaists: they are concerned mainly about the simplification of style, about its liberation from traditional "rhetoric."

The problem of narrative form and genre was no less acute. An attraction to the development of prose appeared already at the end of the 20s. The initial fascination with historical novels quickly waned (Bulgarin, Zagoskin, Lazhechnikov, Polevoy, and others). In the 30s the historical novel undergoes a systematic attack from the critics and belletrists themselves.

Senkovsky declares it "the fruit of the seductive, adulterous relationship between history and the imagination," "the offspring of an art headed for a fall and attempting through counterfeit, indirect means still to have an effect upon man."[76] Odoevsky points to the melodramatic quality of Russian historical novels and considers "this genre tiresome, ridiculed, scorned."[77] Yastrebtsov maintains that "a historical picture in painting is just as unnatural as a historical novel in literature. If one calls such novels historical, then surely they are novels without poetry, i.e., those absurd compositions which pose and are received as novels, although they do not have the literary right to this appellation."[78]

On the other hand, chief attention is directed precisely to the novel, to the large form. The problem of the essence of this genre is discussed actively in periodical articles and reviews. Odoevsky writes an article on A. Stepanov's novel *The Wayside Inn*, in which he reproaches the Russian novelist for "taking the first novelistic incident which came to his mind and piecing all his thoughts and observations together into his work like a patchwork, for foisting his own thoughts onto the characters brought into the scene, for opportunely and inopportunely using anecdotes seen by him in the course of life. No, it is impossible to *make* a poetic composition this way."[79] In his article "What is a Novel," Yastrebtsov says that "the novel has completely conquered the present generation," and defines the novel as "an aesthetic representation of the life of man among men." The problem of the novel becomes the favorite theme of theoretical discussions. Finally, even scholarly dissertations on this theme appear: thus in Kiev in 1844 M. A. Tulov (an instructor in Prince Bezborodko's Nezhin Lyceum) defended his dissertation *On the Novel* "as about one of the basic, typical forms of verbal art."[80]

But in practice the large form does not evolve for a long time; the development of a plot-structure, its transformation into a large, consistently developing story-line, is still beyond the competence of the Russian belletrists of the

30s. The problem of working out the literary language and narrative devices is still so complex that a departure beyond the limits of the small forms is difficult. An ordinary practice for Russian belletrists of the 30s -- the combining of different novellas in the form of "evenings" -- represents a natural transitional step toward the large form. Especial attention is directed toward the details of narrative form: to the means of conducting the narration of the story, to the motivation of transitions from one person to another, to reports about the past, etc. The Russian belletrists learn the treatment of these forms from foreign writers: the names of Sterne, Irving, Zschokke, Balzac, Janin, etc., abound in the texts of articles and tales. To this one must add that the feuilleton develops anew; it is transformed from sketches of manners in the style of Jouy into lively "chatter" on the most diverse themes, sometimes acquiring a quasi-belletristic form (Senkovsky).

The usual form of combining tales is either through framing them with a preface and a conclusion, or through a simple replacement of narrators, which is preceded by an introductory portion describing the very pretext for this narration. This sometimes is employed for the movement of the plot itself: the listeners' remarks or questions are inserted. Thus, Marlinsky's tale "An Evening at a Caucasian Watering-Place in 1824" is an entire chain of tales placed in the mouths of various persons who have gathered together. After two novellas have been related in connection with a conversation struck up at the beginning of the work, one of those present proposes that "each relate some kind of story, some kind of anecdote from his or another's life which would help us while away other evenings and conclude the present one." The unexpectedly simple denouement of the following tale is accompanied by a characteristic remark: "The denouement is too ordinary -- said the mysterious man with a sigh." A "terrifying" tale follows, complete with robbers, a coffin and so on. Different types of "evenings," represented by collections of novellas, continue to be cultivated until the end of the 30s. Thus, in 1837 M. Zhukova's "Evenings at Karpovka" enjoyed great success; in this work we have a complete frame, which motivates the combining of tales, and which itself is developed into small novella (Lyubinka's and Velsky's love).

Given such heightened attention to narrative devices, it is natural to expect the appearance of a specific play with form: the baring of narrative conventions, the comic intrusion of the reader, the intentional retardation of the plot-line by means of various interpolations and digressions, i.e. everything that now is commonly called "Sternianism"[81] and which is always repeated in periods of a departure from old stereotyped forms and the working-out of new forms. Indeed, in Russian belles lettres of the end of the 20s and beginning of the 30s we find these devices in great abundance.

In "The Ordeal" Marlinsky simultaneously dispatches two of his characters from Moscow to Petersburg, and everything that subsequently occurs is contingent upon who will arrive there first. Instead of immediately informing the reader of this, the author fills up the ensuing chapter with a detailed description, in the spirit of the "Flemish School," of the Sennoy market on Christmas eve.[82] The chapter concludes with a conversation with his readers:

> "Pardon me, gentleman writer!" I hear the exclamations of many of my readers, "you have written an entire chapter about the Sytny [sic] market which sooner will arouse an appetite for food than an interest in reading."
>
> "In both instances you are not wrong, kind Sirs!"
>
> "But at least tell us who of our two hussar friends, Grémin or Strelinsky, arrived in the capital?"
>
> "You will not learn this other than by reading two or three chapters, kind Sirs."

In "The Sea-farer Nikitin" the tale is interrupted by a digression in which the charm of sailing on the sea is described with great lyrical, and apparently serious, pathos: ("Then the soul drinks a full cup of heaven's freedom, bathes in the ocean's expanse, and man is changed entirely into a pure, serene, sacred feeling of self-oblivion and ignorance of the world, like an infant just withdrawn from the christening font," etc.). In the most elevated passage this description is suddenly interrupted by the intrusion of the reader: "'O, if I could but entreat fate or bring to life in recollection several such hours! I would... Then I would not at all begin to read your tales,' tells me vexedly one of those readers who unfailingly want the hero of the tale unceasingly and continuously to dance before them on a rope. Let him slip out but for an instant and they start to peek behind the curtains, to skip a chapter ahead: -- 'But where is he? What has become of him? Has he been hurt? Has he been murdered? Has he disappeared without a trace?' -- or what is even worse: 'Is it possible that he has done nothing yet? Is it possible that nothing has happened to him'?" The quarrel with the reader takes up several pages after which follows a phrase wholly in the style of Sterne, whose name Marlinsky mentions quite often: "I am picking up a dropped stitch in the tale." An awareness of similar devices as a means of retardation is confirmed by Marlinsky's letter to his brothers (1833) in which he speaks of *The Frigate Nadezhda*: "Apparently certain chapters were inserted in my work wholly above the specified number as, for example, Kokorin's conversation with the physician. But who knows: did I not wish to arouse the reader's attention through impatience? That also is a secret of art."

In Veltman's *The Immortal Kashchei* (1833) the main hero, Iva, disappears for a long period from the novel until finally the readers recall him: "Mstislav was worthy of the name of Great... -- Let's assume that he was worthy; what is that to us? Where is the Immortal Kashchei? Where is Iva? -- Everything, dear readers, was, is, and will be in its own time and its own place. Your words will hasten neither the impervious sun, nor willful fate, nor the capricious fingers of Bayan the epic bard with his declaiming." More pages pass, and still Iva does not appear. Finally, the author announces: "The reader clearly sees now that not only I, but none of us knows where Iva is. And that is why it is all the better if, to someone's good fortune, he should turn up by royal decree; then I shall continue the ancient tale. But, dear readers, what shall we do until our hero turns up? With what shall I fill the time of uncertainty as to his fate? Where shall I find a distraction for you? Were I Scheherezade..." etc. A declaration follows this: "But do not think, readers, that I am acting with you like a guide, who, while showing the troops the way through the hidden paths of mountains and forests, himself got lost and fled in fear. No, do not fear, readers! The ball which Baba-Yaga gave me rolls on before me. It will lead us to Iva Ivorovich. Here, I give you my hand on it. Let every quill which I shall take in hand again grow back into the wing of the goose from which it was plucked if this is not the truth."

By the middle of the 30s such conversations and quarrels with readers become traditional and, as is apparent from the reviews, tiresome, because everyone is employing them. In M. Voskresensky's novel *He and She* (1836), which generally abounds in all possible devices of play with motivation and narration, and which by that time appear to be stereotypical, there also is a lengthy quarrel with the reader (Part I, chapter VI):

"Listen, Mr. author, you surely are writing a novel for the first time?"

"Quite so, madame, but how did you know?"

"Because you thread the events too crudely. You amused us with this ball at Virgin Field, which, for some reason or another, appeals to you more than other places, such as for example, Kuznetsky bridge, Tverskaya street with its charming boulevard and so on. But meanwhile, at night and in such foul weather, the poor young man in the green cloak with the bamboo cane is still sitting in the Kremlin garden. It is not good to abandon one's heroes in such a disadvantageous position..."

"You are angry that I forced your favorite to sit in the rain

159

at night; but remember, time-honored heroes of novels found themselves in such critical situations. Madame Radcliffe imprisoned them in dungeons, bound them in shackles and starved them. Countess de Genlis forced them to weep as many tears as now would be a drop on Lidin's green manteau. But what about Victor Hugo? And Jules Janin? Lord, spare me such tyrannizing over my heroes!"

Later the play with the reader's impatience continues: "She barely managed to finish, when... I am breaking my pen in vexation (and, of course, I am taking another one, otherwise the novel would never be completed). She barely managed to finish when already... But after all how well everything was starting to go! How proud I was of my hero, how glad I was for all our sex, and what happened? Here's a cold-blooded operator for you! She barely managed to finish when Vladimir was already lying at her feet..."

Something especially should yet be said about forewords. In the 30s they also begin to be employed with the aim of creating a comic effect. Odoevsky ("Princess Mimi," 1834) places the preface in the middle of the tale, thereby interrupting the most important moment of the story: "The door opened and... - But permit me, kind sirs! I think that now is the most appropriate moment to force you to read... *The Preface*. For some time past the custom of writing the preface in the middle of a book has come into usage and already managed to fall into decay. I find this practice splendid, that is, very advantageous for the author" - and there follows a lengthy discussion about how difficult it is to write novels in Russian. This preface concludes with the words: "Hereafter I beg my readers' pardon if I have bored them, trusting to their kind disposition these small, in the full sense of the word, domestic difficulties, which show the props upon which the novelistic wings move. In this instance I am acting like a director of a small provincial theater. Brought to despair by the impatience of the spectators, who are bored by the long intermission, he decided to raise the curtain and show them in fact how difficult it is to transform clouds into a sea, a blanket into a Tsar's royal tent, a housekeeper into a princess, and a negro into a *premier ingénu*. The gracious spectators found this spectacle more engaging than the play itself. I think the same." In Veltman's *The Wanderer* (1831-32) a journey by map is described; this is utilized for the creation of various comic effects (like Xavier de Maistre's "A Journey Around My Room," which imitated Sterne): Thus, here is Europe! You have covered Podoliya with your elbow; ... chase that fly away!... here's Tulchin!... See... O, that was careless!... What a terrible flood in Spain and France!.. That's what comes of putting a glass of water on a map!... But did I ever think that I would knock it from the Pyrenees Mountains with my elbow?" The preface turns up not at the beginning, but in the VI chapter of the first day: "It is very well known to every fancier of reading to what degree every preface is unbearable, particularly when the gentleman writer, still unsure whether or not the reading public will make the effort to read his book, already asks for mercy and compassion for it and excuses its shortcomings with all sorts of circumstances from his personal life. That is why I don't wish to continue the preface," etc.

The cited material is sufficient to convince us that the problem of the literary language and narrative form stands in the center of attention for Russian belletrists of the 30s. The story itself is in the background; in the majority of instances it apparently serves only as a pretext for working out linguistic and narrative devices. Hence the fragmentary quality of plot-line, especially in Veltman. The hero still is completely unpsychologized because he occupies a secondary position in the novel's structure; he is not a structural element of the novel. Marlinsky declares this frankly: "My characters are a private matter." Hence the impression of "contentual poverty" (Kotlyarevsky) which results if one approaches this literature with the demands of a reader reared on Tolstoy and Dostoevsky. We have before us another poetics, one in which the basic organizing role is not played by those structural elements which came to the fore in Russian literature of the ensuing decades.

3

I return to Lermontov. From the historical novel embellished with emotional rhetoric, Lermontov turns to the contemporary society novel whose action develops in Petersburg in 1833 ("Princess Ligovskaya"). Here one can observe a combination of various narrative styles perhaps partly explainable by Lermontov's collaboration with a friend S. A. Raevsky ("The Novel which you and I began has dragged on and it is doubtful whether it will be finished," Lermontov wrote to him in 1838).

The beginning of the novel is written in the style of the "tales of a poor clerk," which already had emerged by then and prepared the way for Gogol's "The Overcoat" and Dostoevsky's first tales:[84] "On the 21st day of December in 1833, at 4 o'clock in the afternoon, as usual a crowd of people thronged along Voznesenky street and, incidentally, a young clerk was walking along... Thus, a certain young clerk was walking along Voznesensky, coming from the department, exhausted by the monotonous work, and dreaming about a decoration and a tasty dinner -- since all clerks dream." A description of his external appéarance follows, at which point the narrator becomes an outside observer: "It was difficult to distinguish his facial features, the reason: his cap, collar, and the twilight."

The description of the house in which the clerk Krasinsky lives belongs to this same style: "First you make your way through a narrow and angular courtyard, through deep snow or watery mud; high pyramids of firewood threaten every moment to crush you by falling; a heavy odor, acrid, repulsive, poisons your breathing; dogs growl at your appearance; pale faces preserving the terrible traces of poverty or profligacy peep through the narrow windows of the lower floor. Finally, after much questioning, you find the desired door, dark and narrow like the door into purgatory. Slipping on the threshold you fly down two steps and your feet land in a puddle which has formed on the stone landing; then, with an unsure hand you feel for the staircase and begin to clamber upward. Ascending to the first floor and stopping on the rectangular landing, you will see several doors around you. But alas! - there is no number on any of them. You begin to knock or ring, and usually a cook comes to the door with a tallow candle, and from behind her can be heard swearing or the crying of children."

In other passages of the novel a high lyrical tone appears reminiscent of Marlinsky and familiar to us from *Vadim*: in Pechorin's face can be discerned "deep traces of the past and wonderful promises of the future...[85] at that moment his enflamed face (the clerk's) was as splendid as a storm... some invisible demon drew their lips and arms together in a wordless embrace, in a wordless kiss." Some of the novel's passages create an impression of parody of this highest style: "Having impressed a hot kiss on her cold virginal forehead" is an ordinary cliche, but something completely different follows upon it: "George sat her down on a chair, ran headlong down the stairs and galloped home." The parodic quality is underscored by an address to the readers immediately thereafter: "Until now, dear readers, you have seen that the love of my heroes has not departed from the rules common to all novels and any incipient love, but then afterwards... O! afterwards you will see and hear marvelous things."

A departure from the high rhetorical style likewise is revealed in the very cautious [sic] use of similes. We even have here something like self-parody; the comparison with an American well at the bottom of which stirs a poisonous crocodile, and which appeared in *Vadim*, is employed comically here and follows a highly prosaic description of the maid: "I cannot endure fat and pock-marked maids with heads smeared with grease or slicked down with kvas, which pastes together and reddens the hair, with arms as rough as yesterday's grated bread, with sleepy eyes, with feet flopping in laceless shoes, heavy of foot and (what is worst of all) with a rectangular waist to which clings a motley-colored house-dress narrower at the bottom than at the top... Such a maid, seated at work in the back room of a respectable house, resembles a crocodile at the bottom of a bright American well."

The transition from *Vadim* to *Princess Ligovskaya* is somewhat analogous to the transition from the early poems and, in particular, from "The Boyar Orsha" to "Sashka." In one instance there is an alternation between a high and comic narrative poem, in the other between an emotional-rhetorical style of narration, wherein the author merges with the hero, and the style of an outside observer or narrator proper. In *Princess Ligovskaya* Lermontov plainly vacillates even in the selection of the material itself as well as in the placing of the hero. The clerk Krasinsky vies with Pechorin for the role of the hero: the narrative advances with difficulty, the story becomes complicated, and the denouement does not take shape.

Likewise characteristic are the narrative details, which are carefully emphasized by the author precisely to create the illusion of the simultaneity of the events taking place and their description or the actual existence of the characters being described and the narrator himself as observer. These are details which were noted above in Voskresensky's novel as devices for playing with narrative form: "Now, after he has removed the greatcoat spattered with snow and has entered into his study, we can freely follow him and describe his outward appearance... Pechorin laid these mortal remains on the table, again sat down in his chair and covered his face with his hands; and although I can discern very well the promptings of a soul in people's faces, for this very reason I can not relate to you his thoughts...[86] Meanwhile some candles were brought and while Varenka fumes and taps a finger against the window, I shall describe for you the room in which we find ourselves... While I was describing the study, Varenka gradually advanced to the table," etc. While not developing these reservations [оговорки] into a comic device, Lermontov seemingly introduces them as the motivation for pauses or for transitions from some characters to others. This testifies to his difficulties in constructing the narrative.

The problem of the novel remained unresolved. The large number of characters (Pechorin, Negurova, the Ligovsky couple, Varenka, the clerk Krasinsky, Branitsky, Gorshenko) and the complex intrigue projected in the chapters written, pave the way toward the large form, whereas, in fact, the novel does not take shape: the intrigue does not create the complications which would connect all the characters. The novel breaks down into a series of scenes and episodes whose linking does not lead to a consistently developing narrative. The need to report about his characters' past, to insert judgements of character, the descriptions of setting, external appearances, etc., clearly trouble the author. The large form is not successful.

From the unitary novel Lermontov arrives at the "chain of tales" (as he himself says in "Maksim Maksimych") united by the figure of Pechorin, thereby freeing himself from the difficulties connected with the development of a large-scale story. In this fashion Lermontov turns to that form which is characteristic of the prose of the 30s; he imparts to it a finished quality, motivating the joining of the tales not only externally but also internally through the unity of the hero. The sequence of events (the hero's general background) required of a unitary novel is lacking; the unity of the hero is not linked to the unity of the intrigue, to the constancy of the remaining characters, to the uniformity of the narrative form, and, at the same time, the tales are welded together firmly by the hero's unvarying presence and participation. Thus concludes the process of elaborating a narrative form which runs through the entire decade, paving the way for the transition to the large form which was realized by the generation of the 40s.

Indeed, precisely those narrative problems were resolved in *A Hero of Our Time* which were at the center of belles lettres of the 30s, and hereby too was liquidated that tiresome play with form which had turned into the naive cliche which we traced in the works of Marlinsky, Veltman, Odoevsky, and Voskresensky. The new task lay precisely in finding satisfying motivations for the descriptions, character judgements, digressions, the introduction of the narrator, etc. We find all of this in Lermontov.

Having dropped the idea of constructing a unitary story, Lermontov thereby rid himself of the need to introduce a biography of his characters into the novel (*Vorgeschichte*). Breaking up the novel ("the composition," as Lermontov called it) into tales, he made his hero a static figure. In place of the customary chronology, in which the hero's life is set forth, we have another kind of sequence connected not with the hero but with the author: from his encounter with Maksim Maksimych to the tale about Pechorin, from the tale to the accidental meeting with him, from the meeting to his "journal." The secondary sequence (the story of the author's acquaintance with the hero) plays a structural role, and the basic sequence (the hero's life) is so displaced that even after reading the entire novel it is difficult to arrange the reported events in chronological order.

Thus, the position of the author as the basic narrator of the first two tales ("Bela" and "Maksim Maksimych") is wholly established and motivated by the fact that he is writing "not a tale, but travel notes" ("Bela"), and at the same time is also motivated by the chronological displacement of the events. Pechorin's "Journal," which in a certain sense is his *Vorgeschichte* (with respect to the first two tales), in fact does not have this meaning because the unity of the story has been destroyed. The events related in the "Journal" are perceived by us without any temporal connection with what was related earlier. In general we know nothing about Pechorin's past; we do not even know why he has turned up in the Caucasus. At first Lermontov thought about reporting this in passing: the first entry in the manuscript of "Princess Mary" concludes with the words: "But now I am sure that at the first chance she will ask who I am and why am I here in the Caucasus. They probably will tell her the *frightful story of the duel* and especially its cause, which is known to a few here." But Lermontov crossed this out, apparently finding such a hint at the past superfluous.

Thus, *A Hero of Our Time* is not a tale, not a novel, but travel notes to which a portion of Pechorin's "Journal" has been attached. This motivation has special meaning for "Bela": owing to it the descriptive material is established not as an accidental appendage to the tale, not as "landscape," but as a perfectly natural and essential element of narration. Maksim Maksimych's tale proves to be the result of a conversation struck up on the road. It is employed for the movement of the plot-line itself: the tale is retarded not by chance digressions, and not by the author's or reader's comic intrusion, but by the very state of things. For example, Maksim Maksimych does not relate everything all at once but with a hiatus: the first part during the stop at the station near Gud-Gora, and the second during the lay-over on the road to Kobi. Thus, the tale about Bela was woven into the description of the journey from Tiflis to Kobi station: the description entered into the tale as a structural element. The traditional landscape introduction is fused into the form itself: from the description of the Koyshaursky valley to the description of the road itself and hence to the acquaintanceship with Maksim Maksimych; from the acquaintanceship to the conversation, from the conversation to the tale. "You probably have had a lot of adventures?" - this question accomplishes the transition to the story proper. Moreover, the author also motivates his own curiosity: "I wanted terribly to draw out of him some little tale, -- a desire common to all travelers and note-taking people."[87]

The movement of the story proper is guided by the listener constantly posing questions ("How did that happen?"... "And what was his name?"... "And did he live long with you?..." etc.). The descriptive moments of the tale are motivated precisely by the listener's questions of this sort: "How do they celebrate a wedding?... And what did she sing, do you recall?"

A concern for motivation also is revealed in the fact that Lermontov makes a special notation about Kazbich's song, which once more stresses the author's position as a professional writer: "I beg the reader's pardon for transposing Kazbich's song into verse; it was, of course, transmitted to me in prose. But habit is second nature."

With Maksim Maksimych's words "Yes, they were happy," the tale about Bela apparently is concluded: "How boring this is!, I involuntarily exclaimed.

165

Indeed, I expected a tragic denouement and then to deceive my hope so unexpectedly!" A lengthy description of early morning follows ("We came out of the hut," etc.) as well as the continuation of the journey, which suddenly is interrupted by the author's question, directly addressed to the reader: "But perhaps you wish to know the conclusion of Bela's story? First of all, I am writing not a tale but travel notes: consequently I cannot force the staff-captain to tell his story before he, in fact, began to tell his story. Thus, either wait or, if you wish, turn ahead several pages; only I do not advise you to do this because the crossing of Krestovaya Mountain (or, as the scholar Ham calls it, le Mont St.-Christophe) is worthy of your curiosity. And so," -- and a description of the crossing follows. The plot-line retardation is motivated by the travel-notes form itself.

As we see, Lermontov's attention really is directed at the motivation of narrative devices. The description of Koyshaursky valley and the crossing through Kobi are motivated; the retardation is motivated; Maksim Maksimych's story is motivated, and even the movement of the story itself. Finally, Maksim Maksimych himself is transformed from a traditional, always more or less conventional story-teller, into a literary personality. His position is reinforced both by the fact that he is a participant in the events linked to Pechorin's personality, and by the fact that he is granted certain psychological features which contrast with the personality of the main hero. Lermontov specifically emphasizes this at the end of the tale by bringing Maksim Maksimych to the foreground, almost making him the main hero: "Confess, however, that Maksim Maksimych is a man worthy of respect?... If you will admit this, then I shall be rewarded fully for my perhaps too lengthy story." This is a characteristic "false ending" (V. Shklovsky's term) which, in effect, emphasizes the fact that Maksim Maksimych is a secondary character, a traditional story-teller, whose role is specially motivated and reinforced this time in order to conceal an ordinary device and thus to achieve "naturalness."

"Maksim Maksimych" is a transitional tale which prepares the transition to the "journal." The author's encounter with his hero occurs here; the scene is sufficiently sharp with respect to its formal paradoxical quality, but it is so well-grounded by Lermontov that from a device characteristic of a play with form it is transformed here into a natural situation motivated by the entire course of events.[88] In essence, Lermontov needs this encounter in order to motivate a detailed description of Pechorin's external appearance (once more we see how Lermontov is concerned for the motivation of this kind of feature)- otherwise he would have had to reject completely such a description or place it in the mouth of Maksim Maksimych, which would have been difficult.

It is characteristic that in this description Lermontov maintains the tone of an outside observer who makes inferences about a character only from external features: "His gait was careless and lazy, but I noticed that he did not swing his arms - a sure sign of a certain reticence of character." And immediately after this comes a special reservation: "However, these are personal remarks based on my own observations and in no way do I wish to force you to believe in them blindly." Then there is yet another reservation: "All these remarks came to mind, perhaps, only because I knew certain details of his life and, perhaps, his appearance would produce a completely different impression on another person. But since you will not hear about him from anyone other than myself, you perforce must be satisfied with this portrayal."

In the manuscript text a portion of the description is crossed out, i.e. precisely that part in which Lermontov, departing from the role of an outside observer, began to speak directly about Pechorin's character, thereby somewhat approaching his old manner ("Pechorin belonged to the crowd, and if he did not become either a villain or a saint, it was, I'm certain, out of laziness"). This example clearly shows how strictly Lermontov maintains his position of an objective narrator here, and how he does not permit himself to depart from his basic motivation. Here he not only does not merge with his character, he not only abstains from any sort of lyricism, but even intentionally underscores his position as a professional writer who has happened upon some interesting literary material: "Recently I learned that Pechorin died while returning from Persia. This news made me very happy: it gave me the right to publish these notes." The ending of this tale is again devoted to the person of Maksim Maksimych; a correspondence with the ending of "Bela" results, or yet another false ending.

Earlier I pointed out the play with prefaces which are placed in the middle and sometimes (as in Odoevsky) serve as a means of plot retardation. Lermontov, in essence, does the very same thing: the preface comes just before Pechorin's "journal."[89] In line with its general character this preface relates not only to the "journal" itself, but even to the entire book; but its appearance in the middle is motivated sufficiently by the very transition to the "journal." Here, as in other instances, Lermontov employs a device traditional for Russian belles lettres of the 30's, but established his motivation in such a way that the purely formal role of the device is concealed.

The journal itself consists of three tales ("Taman," "Princess Mary" and "The Fatalist") of varying types. "Taman" is a tale oriented toward plot, as is "Bela." There are no special signs of a diary here; the story has the usual form of a tale (told in the first person). On the contrary, there are details which impart to it the character of a pure narrative, a narration addressed to listeners: "*I confess*, I have a strong prejudice against all blind persons, all one-eyed people... And so, I began to examine the blind boy's face; but what *am I supposed* to discern in a face which has no eyes?... *I confess*, no matter how hard I tried," etc. The ending also is typical for the tale: "What became of the old woman and the poor blind boy -- I don't know. And what do I care for human joys and calamities, me, a traveling officer, and, moreover, one with traveling orders on official duty!..."

One must assume that in the first draft, which has not come down to us, these signs were even clearer; the manuscript text of "Maksim Maksimych" contains a notation at the end which reads: "I went over Pechorin's notes and noticed in several passages that he was preparing them for publication, without which, of course, I would not have decided to abuse the trust of the staff-captain. Indeed, in several passages Pechorin does address himself to the readers." Clearly this must have served as the motivation for the fact that not everywhere in Pechorin's "journal" are the features of a diary preserved as such.

The very idea of the "journal" is not, evidently, the basic design determining the character of the style, - rather it is a motivation. Lermontov decided to free himself from all unmotivated utterances about his characters; he even decided against reporting what any one of them (this or that one) was thinking or had thought. Hence the emphasis upon his position as a travelling litterateur, the introduction of a special narrator as a personal witness of events, and, finally, the "journal." We thus have three "I's": the author, Maksim Maksimych, and Pechorin. These "I's" proved to be imperative because otherwise it would have been necessary to make the author a witness of all the events and thereby limit greatly the narrative possibilities.

For all of Lermontov's concern about motivation, certain details proved to elude it, which is almost unavoidable in a first-person tale. Maksim Maksimych is insistently obliged to eavesdrop on others' conversations (as is Pechorin in "Taman," but there it is motivated by suspicion): Azamat's conversation with Kazbich, Pechorin's conversation with Bela ("I was walking past and glanced in the window"). Lermontov was forced to motivate Pechorin's long self-characterizing description, the style of which is utterly unlike Maksim Maksimych's style, by the fact that Pechorin's words were "etched" in his memory; in "Taman" the text of the song is motivated by having Pechorin remember it word for word, etc. One passage in "The Fatalist," which relates Vulich's death, remained wholly unmotivated: "Vulich was walking alone along a dark street; the drunken Cossack, who had hacked the pig to pieces, collided with him; perhaps he would have passed by without even noticing him had not Vulich suddenly stopped and said: "Whom are you looking for, old man?" "You!," answered the Cossack, striking him with a sabre and cleaving him from the shoulder almost to the heart..." Clearly, no one but Vulich himself could have related this, but Vulich managed to say only three words: "He was right." Such instances reveal the motivational nature of these "I's": Maksim Maksimych in "Bela," Pechorin in "Taman" and "The Fatalist."

"Taman" is a tale of plot. Pechorin is not so much a hero here as a narrator; the plot itself is developed by the material of his observations, feelings, and reflections. The entire piece is constructed on the movement from the first hint that it was "unclean" (the word is employed in its dual sense) in the house where Pechorin decided to go, to the concluding catastrophe. It is characteristic of Lermontov that this tale was developed not by combining various elements which could be expanded equally into a large form (as in Pushkin's "The Snowstorm," "The Shot," and in "The Stationmaster," where one senses a compression of the story material), but out of a small episode which was developed to the limits of the tale. This, evidently, is what forced Chekhov into raptures over "Taman." The tale is made up of a small, undistinguished and inconclusive adventure in which its every word, every movement is sensed. Lermontov showed himself to be a master of the short form here; it is not for nothing that in his circle of friends he was praised as a narrator of anecdotes.

In "Princess Mary," as a portion of Pechorin's diary, aphorisms and paradoxes occur naturally. The traditional society tale with balls and duels is raised in its significance because the hero is psychologized. He is motivated as a personality, as a character, which neither Marlinsky nor Odoevsky and Pavlov succeeded in doing; indeed, their attention could not have been directed yet at this feature ("my characters are a private matter," wrote Marlinsky). True, the elaborate psychologization to which literary characters in Tolstoy or Dostoevsky are subjected is still non-existent in Lermontov; the impression of a "personality" and, moreover, a "typical one" is created not by a detailed analysis of spiritual states, not by a diversity of feelings and thoughts, but by the very make-up of the aphorisms, conversations, and reflections of the hero. Thoughts find refuge in Pechorin's diary which Lermontov had long since placed in the mouths of his heroes. Thus, his tirade against himself ("Yes, such was my fate since childhood") is taken directly from the drama *Two Brothers*. In this sense "Princess Mary" in general belongs to the tradition of aphoristic literature, with this distinction: here this material, as everything in *A Hero of Our Time,* is firmly fused into the tale as a descriptive element.

Interlocutors are necessary for dialogue, and Grushnitsky and Doctor Werner appear in this capacity in "Princess Mary." Like Maksim Maksimych,

Grushnitsky is a secondary character to whom a very modest position would have been allotted in the old tale. Lermontov enhances his position here, making him a parodic, contrasting character, and forcing him to participate in a most intimate way in all the events. The secondary, dependent quality of this figure, incidentally, is revealed in the fact that they both utter the very same phrase, notwithstanding their underscored contrast. In the first entry Pechorin says that the wives of the local authorities "are accustomed in the Caucasus to meet *an ardent heart under a numbered button and an educated intellect under a white service-cap.*" Somewhat later (in the very same entry) in a conversation with Pechorin, Grushnitsky says about the aristocracy:"This proud nobility looks at us soldiers as at savages. And what is it to them if there is *an intellect under a numbered service-cap and a heart under a heavy cloak?*" The dialogue is constructed according to Marlinsky's system in the form of a chain of puns and witticisms, but Lermontov, compressing it, makes it quick and brief and does not develop it through a special play on words.

It also must be pointed out that the novel is constructed on the paradoxical situation of "I do not love you"; against the background of the traditional society tale this appears to be a departure or somewhat of an innovation. This paradoxicalness lends a sharpness to all the situations right up to the duel. Lermontov took the original situation of *Evgeny Onegin* and constructed an entire tale upon it. Vera appears as the motivation for the duel; it is no accident that she disappears without a trace as soon as her plot function has been fulfilled. It is natural that an entire line of tales and novels, including Turgenev's early tales, develops precisely from "Princess Mary" as the largest-form tale to have solved the problem of "character."

And so, in *A Hero of Our Time* Lermontov uniquely synthesizes those formal quests which are chracteristic of Russian belles lettres of the 30s. He puts the literary language in order, renouncing lyrical pathos as well as a fascination with dialecticisms, word-play, etc. S. Burachek was not entirely wrong when, indignant at Lermontov's novel, he called it an "epigram" consisting of uninterrupted sophisms and "the ideal of light reading." Indeed, after Marlinsky, Veltman, Odoevsky, and Gogol, where everything was still so labored, so heterogeneous, so unmotivated and therefore so "unnatural," *A Hero of Our Time* looks like the first "light" book; a book in which formal problems are concealed beneath careful motivation and which, therefore, was able to create the illusion of "naturalness" and to arouse an interest in pure reading. Attention to motivation becomes the basic formal slogan of Russian literature from the 40s through the 60s ("realism"). The Russian psychological novel becomes possible after *A Hero of Our Time*, although from Lermontov's prose a direct literary-historical line leads not to the novel, but to Turgenev's novella-tales and to the tales of Chekhov.

- - - - - - - - - -

Lermontov died early, but this fact bears no relation to the historical work which he accomplished, and changes nothing in the resolution of the literary-historical problem which interests us. It was necessary to sum up the classical period of Russian poetry and to prepare the transition to the creation of a new prose. History demanded it -- and it was accomplished by Lermontov.

NOTES

Quotations from Lermontov's works are taken from the text printed in the Government Publishing House (Leningrad) edition of his works, verified anew against the original texts by K. I. Khalabaev and myself. Incidentally, in verifying the texts it was discovered that certain manuscripts of the Lermontov Museum (currently located in the Pushkin House) are not originals as has been thought (see the Academy Edition, Vol. V, pp. 26-32), but copies. Of the 23 notebooks of the Lermontov Museum the wholly original manuscripts are: I, II, III, IV, V, VI, VII, VIII, IX, X, XI, XVI, XVIII, XXII, XXIII. The composition of the remaining notebooks is as follows:

Notebook XII ("The Boyar Orsha") - an authorized copy.

Notebook XIII ("The Novice") - pp. I - 337 comprise an authorized copy; the remainder is an original manuscript (the title page, epigraph, and page 338 to the end).

Notebook XIV ("A Fairytale for Children") - a rough-draft manuscript; a fair, authorized copy of the original.

Notebook XV (Poems) - a miscellany: Nos. I - I4 ("The Mermaid, "The Prisoner," "The Angel," "When the Yellowing Cornfield Waves," "A Wanderer's Prayer," "The Neighbor," "We Parted," "A Branch of Palestine," "Two Giants," "The Dying Gladiator," "A Wish," "In the Untamed North," "The Sail," "For worldly Shackles") and Nos. I8 - 20 ("The Last House-Warming," "The Dagger," "A Captive Knight") are copies; the rest are original manuscripts.

Notebook XVII (*The Spaniards*) - an authorized copy.

Notebook XIX (*Two Brothers*) - an authorized copy.

Notebook XX (Poems) - Nos. I - I05 are copies; the rest (Nos. 106 - II8) are original manuscripts.

Notebook XXI (Verse and Narratives) - a miscellany: Nos. 3 ("Kally"), 5 ("A Dead Man's Love"), and 6 ("In the Untamed North") are copies; the rest are original manuscripts.

Thus the information on sources given in the notes to the Academy Edition and the description of Lermontov's manuscripts does not always prove to be correct, and many manuscript facsimiles ("The Boyar Orsha,"

"A Fairytale for Children," "A Dead Man's Love," "In the Untamed North," *The Spaniards*) are photographs not of original manuscripts but of copies.

. . . .

1. *Biografiia F. N. Tiutcheva* (M., 1886), p. 79 and thereafter. In his verse I. Aksakov sharply departs from the Pushkinian style and is a precursor of Nekrasov (see my article "Nekrasov" in the journal *Nachala*, 1922, No. 2, and in the collection *Skvoz' literaturu*, 1923.

2. Shevyryov noted the same thing: "It is pleasant to note that the poet subordinates his muse not principally to just anyone else's muse but to many, and this diversity of influences is already a good guarantee for the future" (*Moskvitianin*, 1841, part II, No. 4, p. 536).

3. In the article "On the Tendency of Our Poetry, Especially Lyric, in the Last Decade" (*Mnemozina*, 1824, part II, pp. 29 - 44) V. Kyukhelbeker, acknowledging that "among us the elegy and the epistle have supplanted the ode," sets as his task ("As a son of the fatherland I assume an obligation to boldly state the truth") to prove that the ode alone completely satisfies all the demands of lyric poetry ("in general lyric poetry is nothing but the uncommon, i. e. powerful, free, inspired exposition of the writer's own feelings") and that is why "it doubtlessly occupies the foremost position in lyric poetry or, better said, it alone wholly merits the name of lyric poetry." Having portrayed the essence of the elegy and epistle in ironic outline as lower genres, Kyukhelbeker poses the question: "Have we gained by exchanging the ode for the elegy and the epistle?" It is evident from this remarkable article what an urgent problem the question of lyric genres was at the time.

4. "Sasha Chyorny" is a parody of Nekrasov's "Sasha" (1856) - tr.

5. V. Zhirmunsky ("On the Problem of the Formal Method" - the foreword to the Russian translation of O. Walzel's book *The Problem of Form in Poetry* [Petrograd: "Academiia," 1923]), objecting to the theoretical positions of OPOYAZ and insisting on the explanation of change in literary styles by a change in "world perception" or "by a general shift in spiritual culture" (as if art does not participate in this shift but only "reflects" it) says that "the most diverse tendencies can arise through contrast," whereas "actually we observe in the change of styles... one dominant artistic tendency marking the appearance of a new style as a self-contained unity or system of mutually-conditioned devices." In point of fact, however, there is no such propitious order in the living historical process. Precisely "the most diverse tendencies" arise and coexist, whose correlation also forms an epoch in the genuine his-

torical meaning of this word. That tendency which is successful becomes dominant for a time. Commencing with the sharpest contrast with respect to the customary canon, and thereby gaining for itself a revolutionary position, henceforth it softens the sharpness of its own principles and makes them acceptable, and later even customary. Its dominance is already a sign of its decline. An epoch is created not at the moment of victory (generally an abstract moment to a significant degree), but by the very process of struggle and coming into being in which the revolutionary (romantic) tendency is inspired by the pathos of contrast with regard to the specific canon, and other tendencies develop on the basis of a more complex historical dialectic. If this kind of process seems "mechanical" to Zhirmunsky, then his construct, in which art submits to external stimuli and skips from one "self-contained unity" to another, seems to me even more mechanical and an oversimplification of the facts.

6. V. Fisher also speaks about this in the article "The Poetics of Lermontov" (the Jubilee collection *Venok M. Iu. Lermontovu,* 1914, pp. 198 - 199): "He has details in readiness - set phrases, epithets, antitheses; the question is where to apply them. Ideas and plot-lines change in Lermontov's imagination, but the basic elements of form recur and seek an appropriate application." Compare in V. Spasovich's book *Baironizm u Pushkina i Lermontova* (Vilnius, 1911), p. 50 and thereafter.

7. A. I. Odoevsky devotes several characteristic lines to him in the poem "Poetry" (1839):

> Пусть наш протей Сенковский, твой гонитель,
> Пути ума осыпав остротой,
> Катается по прозе вечно гладкой
> И сеет слух, что век проходит твой!
> Не знает он поэзии святой,
> Поэзии страдательной и сладкой!

> Let our Proteus Senkovsky, your persecutor,
> Having strewn the paths of the mind with wit,
> Roll along on eternally facile prose
> And sow the rumor that your age is passing!
> He does not know sacred poetry,
> Sweet and suffering poetry!

8. Indeed, this principle of arrangement also lay at the basis of almost all the subsequent editions up to that of P. Viskovatov (1891). S. Dudyshkin writes in the notes to the 1860 edition (in two volumes): "The first part (and

174

the first volume) includes everything that Lermontov published or acknowledged as suitable for printing; the second part (and volume) will contain all of Lermontov's poetry, from the initial attempts to the complete formation of the Lermontovian verse line and prose." P. Efremov also speaks in these same words (the 1873 edition): "Our intention was above all that the reader should encounter *that* Lermontov whom he himself wished to be in the eyes of society, and for this reason we have designated as the *first volume* the collection of all those works which Lermontov himself published or acknowledged as suitable for publication. To these we have added only a few works principally from the *last two years* of his poetic activity, works which, although they were not printed during the poet's own life, are distinguished by high merit.... For that reason all the preliminary, internal, so to speak, work of the writer-- from the first attempts of almost a child to the complete formation of the Lermontovian verse line and prose--went into the composition of the *second volume.*" It is characteristic that already in the 1887 edition Efremov declared that he "omitted two unfinished tales as not of vital interest for the majority of readers, and excerpts from the verse written by the poet in cadet school or soon after leaving it were significantly abridged."

In the editions edited by A. Vvedensky, I. Boldakov, and N. Bukovsky, the same principle of selection was retained. P. Viskovatov arranged Lermontov's works differently: by type (lyric poetry, narrative poems, dramas, prose), preserving the chronology inside each volume; moreover, he published much new material. By this time the problem of printing Lermontov's youthful pieces already had lost its acuteness. Nonetheless Viskovatov considers it necessary to justify himself in the foreword: "Doubtless people will be found ready to reproach me for printing almost every line written by the poet, every imperfect work of a youth which the writer himself would not have published. But in answer to this I will remark: who can take upon himself the liberty of making a selection? Let us assume that one can say what is really good and bad; but how many works occupy a middle ground between these extremes and who is the judge here? The poet himself, they will tell me. Go ahead and print what he himself acknowledged worthy of printing. But the poet, in the edition published in 1840 during his lifetime, included only 28 of his poems and after that a few others in periodical publications." It is remarkable that Viskovatov, in printing Lermontov's youthful verses "corrected" a great deal in them, evidently wishing to present them to the reader in a more acceptable form.

8a. *Marlinsky* also attempted to write narrative poems but, convinced of the futility of his work, gave up poetry and turned to prose. His own acknowledgements, made in 1831 in the foreword of the narrative poem "An-

175

drei, Prince of Pereyaslavl," are very interesting: "Gentlemen poets know how contemporary narrative poems are written, and for this reason it is pointless for me to expatiate on how I discarded thoughts for lack of rhyme or rhymes for the absence of thought; of ten pictures begun scarcely two were half-completed and I wished, in accord with the license of the verbal guild to sew the conclusions together with blank verse as with white threads.... It was not that I denied all the virtues in this tale: there are fresh scenes in it, successful similes, ringing poetic lines, wholly unborrowed thoughts; ... but all the same I was convinced that it would lack that magnitude, that wholeness which marks the physiognomy of works of genius, and I gave up a field in which I was not fated to outstrip many. Strictly speaking, I did not forever renounce for myself the charming chatterbox of poetry who had granted me so many sweet hours of oblivion from suffering; but now I am content with strolls alone and not with distant journeys with her.... I should be very glad if my confession should serve as a lesson for many young poets." Incidentally, we find the first line of Lermontov's "The Sail" ("A solitary sail shimmers white") precisely in this poem (chapter I, stanza 15).

9. See B. Neyman's articles in *Zhurnal ministerstva narodnogo prosveshcheniia* (1915, No. 4 and 1917, No. 3) and in *Izvestiia otdela russkogo iazyka i slovesnosti* (Vol. XIX, 1914, Book I).

I0. In sending his narrative poem "Brother Brigands" to P. Vyazemsky, Pushkin writes: "Certain lines recall the translation of 'The Prisoner of Chillon.' For me this is unfortunate. Zhukovsky and I accidentally merged; my fragment was written at the end of 1821." (1823, *Correspondence*, I, 86). Such "coincidences" once more reveal the presence of extra-individual laws in any historical process, including even the history of art.

11. See V. Zhirmunsky's article "The Byronism of Pushkin as a Literary Historical Problem," *Pushkinskii sbornik pamiati Prof. S. A. Vengerova*, (Gosizdat, 1923).

12. An interesting article by T., "On the Writing of Lyric Poetry" (*Vestnik Evropy*, 1810, chapter LI, No. 10, pp. 128-133) is devoted to the problem of the lyric in general and of lyrical genres in particular. The main genres of lyric poetry are the hymn, the ode, the song, and the idyll: "It seems that to these it would be possible to add the elegy too." On the lyric in general it is said: "Be that as it may, singing properly belonged only to the writing of lyric poetry alone, for the epic and tragic verse lines were uttered similar to the present-day *recitative.* In order to more clearly picture the nature of lyric verse, one must turn to the beginning of song. It arises from a fullness of heart and pours forth in variable, measured tones, corresponding to the disposition of our soul... Lyric verse naturally must be more pleasant

and euphonious than any other composition; they must be divided into parts or stanzas, not too long so that they are accommodated by the ear, and not too short so that they do not bore through frequent repetition." A. Galich's classification of lyric genres is unique ("An Attempt at the Refined," 1825). He distinguishes three main types: the ode, the elegy, and the romance or the ballad. He calls the song a "minor ode" divested of "convulsive frenzies." By elegy he means "melancholy or joyful singing aroused by recollection." The epigram is a type of elegy (when "feeling holds firm in the consciousness until the poet gives *only one judgement* of it"): it "can take all forms so that its use for satire, an inscription, and so on, is wholly accidental." The romance or ballad is a special "romantic elegy" with an element of the epic: "the ideal of the song elevated to the epic." The striving to reduce the basic genres to two types--the ode and the elegy--and to consider the rest as their sub-types is noticeable here.

13. For the details see my article "Pushkin's Path to Prose," (*Sbornik pamiati S. A. Vengerova* [Petersburg, Gosizdat, 1923]).

14. See V. Mendel'son's article "Folk Motifs in the Poetry of Lermontov," *Venok M. Iu. Lermontovu*, pp. 165-195.

15. See the Russian translation of the third part of E. Duchesne's book entitled *Poeziia Lermontova v ee otnoshenii k russkoi i zapadnoevropeiskim literaturam* (Kazan,,1914) [*Michel Iourievitch Lermontov*, (Paris, 1910)] ; the articles by S. V. Shuvalov,"The Influence of Russian and European Poetry on Lermontov's Creative Work," and M. N. Rozanov, "Byronic Motifs in Lermontov's Creative Work" in the jubilee collection *Venok M. Iu. Lermontovu* (M., 1914) and S. I. Rodzevich's book *Lermontov kak romanist* (Kiev, 1914).

16. *Marlinsky* very definitely motivates his use of the material of others: "I borrow turns of speech, speech forms, proverbial and colloquial sayings not from the French alone, but from all the Europeans. Yes, I wish to renew, to diversify the Russian language, and for this I take my gold from the mountain and from the mud with both hands, from wherever I may encounter it, from wherever I may catch it. What kind of false thought is still lodged in many, as if there were Gallicisms, Germanisms, Satanisms in the world? There have been none and there are none!.... Once and for all--I bend the language in various ways intentionally and not by error; I take ready-made material from foreigners if it exists; if not, I invent it; I change the cases for shadings of movement or the refinement of a word.... In any author I will find a hundred passages taken entirely from others; another can find as many; and this does not hinder them from being original because they looked at the things differently." (A letter to his brothers in 1835, from I. Zamotin, *Romantic Idealism*, p. 206). Musset speaks about the same phenomenon very wittily in

the narrative poem "Namouna," similar in construction to Byron's "Beppo:"

Byron, me direz-vous, m'a servi de modèle
Vous ne savez donc pas qu'il imitait Pulci?
Lisez les Italiens, vous verrez s'il les vole.
Rien n'appartient à rien, tout appartient à tous.
Il faut être ignorant comme un maître d'école
Pour se flatter de dire une seule parole
Que personne ici-bas n'ait pu dire avant vous.
C'est imiter quelqu'un que de planter des choux.

17. A. de Vigny speaks very clearly about this need for *another's material* in the foreword to his translation of Shakespeare's *Othello* (the translation was done in 1829; the foreword was written in 1839): "Sans doute, nos grands maîtres nous ont laissé un magnifique trésor national; mais enfin il n'est pas inépuisable, et l'on sentira de plus en plus la nécessité d'ajouter des tableaux aux nôtres, comme à l'Ecole francaise nos musées ont joint les chefs-d'oeuvre des Ecoles italiennes, flamandes et espagnoles." (*Théâtre complet de A. de Vigny* [Paris: Charpentier, 1841], p. 5).

18. To illustrate I quote from N. Polevoy's article in "The New Painter of Society and Literature," 1830, No. I9, October (the supplement to *Moskovskii telegraf,* p. 332): "For a long time our poets have been complaining about the lack of subjects for Poetry. This compels them to sing one and the same thing, to relate a *tiresome fairytale* about the past, about tears, and again about a dozen odds and ends, a hundred times refurbished and worn out. Poetic poverty has reached the ultimate degree in the current year! Poets, who previously have written one hundred verses in a year, who sometimes broke out with narratives running to 20 little pages, grew dumb in 1830, writing 20 or 30 verses apiece, so that the Misters Shevyryovs and Trilynnys of necessity take the place of our most celebrated poets." See likewise my article "Pushkin's Path to Prose" (*Pushkinskii sbornik pamiati Prof. S. A. Vengerova*, 1923).

19. I underline the places with abbreviated anacruses and with intervals between stresses, which distinguish them from the general meter.

20. The same is in Byron: "I cannot lose a world for thee, / But would not lose thee for a world," "On earth thy love was such to me; / It fain would form my hope in heaven!" "Oh! what are a thousand living loves / To that which cannot quit the dead?," etc. [These are the concluding lines to, respectively, "Stanzas Written in Passing the Ambracian Gulf," "To Thyrza," "One Struggle More and I Am Free." - tr.]

21. See "Byronism in Pushkin and Lermontov" in V. Spasovich's book

(Wilno, 1911, p. 53). Compare the concluding lines of Lamartine's poem "Le solitaire": "Ainsi plus le temple est vide, / Plus l'écho sacré retentit."

22. Glancing through Lamartine I found the source of Tyutchev's poem "As the ocean embraces the terrestrial sphere," the originality of which until now, it seems, has not been suspect. In its basic "imagistic" part this poem goes back to Lamartine's meditation "Les étoiles" (*Nouvelles méditations poétiques* [Paris, 1823], pp. 28 - 53), namely to that part where night is described:

> Cependant, la nuit marche, et sur *l'abîme immense*
> Tous ces mondes flottants gravitent en silence,
> *Et nous-même, avec eux emportes dans leur cours,*
> *Vers un port inconnu nous avancons toujours!*
> Souvent, pendant la nuit, au souffle du zéphire,
> *On sent la terre aussi flotter comme un navire.*
>
> . . . .
> *Et l'homme, sur l'abîme ou sa demeure flotte,*
> *Vogue avec volupté sur la foi du pilote!*

From this large, minutely detailed and eloquently developed system, Tyutchev, in keeping with his own method, creates a small fragment using Lamartine's material.

23. "Pure as the prayer which Childhood wafts above" (Canto I, 6).

24. The same simile is in the poem "Incline to Me" (1830):

> Ты помнишь? Серебристая луна,
> Как ангел средь отверженных, меж туч
> Блуждала .....

> Do you recall? The silvery moon
> Like an angel amidst outcasts,
> Roamed between clouds...

This simile often is encountered. Compare in P. Mashkov's tale "The Boarding - School Girl" (*Povesti*, P. Mashkov, St. Petersburg, 1833, p. 90). "Black clouds, like crowds of criminal angels cast out of heaven, quickly flew through the air."

25. This is noted in N. Brodsky's article, "The Poetic Confession of a Member of the Russian Intelligentsiia of the 1830s and 40s," in the Jubilee collection *Venok Lermontovu*, p. 69.

179

26. It is characteristic that the theme of "a prisoner before execution" was developed by Polezhaev also independently, not in the form of a simile. Such is the poem "The Condemned One," which begins with the words: I am condemned to an infamous execution," and concludes with reflections on his lot and the sudden exclamation:

> But what? A crowd of people
> Already is boiling on the square
> I hear: "Prisoner, come out!"
> I am ready, I go!... Forgive me, nature!
> Hangman, lead me to the execution!...

27. In Byron: "Blind, boundless, mute and motionless." In the academy edition there is an erroneous rendering: boundless as *"nebrezhnyi"*.

28. Compare in the poem "Night, II" (1830): "My heart was constricted by a strange half-light, mid-way between joy and grief."

29. The traditional attribution of the indicated stanzas of "Sashka" to Polezhaev (Viskovatov, N. Kotlyarevsky, D. Abramovich) is completely illegitimate. Polezhaev died not in "foreign fields" but in Moscow; moreover, he died in 1838, whereas the narrative is dated 1836. Evidently these stanzas either relate to A. Odoevsky, in which case the narrative was written not earlier than 1839 (which is improbable since the realia of the narrative do not tally with his biography), or they relate to another person (but, of course, not to Polezhaev); consequently, their appearance in the poem "To the Memory of A. I. Odoevsky" is explained by Lermontov's customary transfer of material from one piece to another. It is most likely that the hero of "Sashka" is a purely literary character who does not coincide with any specific person.

30. K. A. Shimkevich first pointed to the close connection between the styles of Lermontov and Podolinsky in his report "On the Question of the Sources of 'The Demon'," read in the spring of 1923 at the "Society for the Study of Artistic Literature" in the Russian Institute for the History of the Arts.

31. Compare in "The Boyar Orsha": "The bloody worm is a grave dweller."

32. Compare in the poem "Solitude" (1830):

> Никто о том не покрушится,
> И будут (я уверен в том)
> О смерти больше веселиться,
> Чем о рождении моем.

No one will grieve for that,
And they will (I am sure of this)
Enjoy themselves more at my death
Than at my birth.

33. A. de Vigny speaks about this in his "Lettre à Lord***," which was written concerning the staging of *Othello* (1829) in his translation, and represents an entire treatise on the theory of the drama. A translation of this "letter" was printed in *Moskovskij telegraf* in 1830 (No. 24, pp. 423-463). Here is the passage I have in mind: "Prose presents an important failing, all too obvious on the stage, when one translates epic passages into it: it seems turgid, high-flown, melodramatic, whereas the verse line is more elastic and bends to all forms; we are not surprised even when it flies, for *when it moves we feel that it has wings.*"

34. Lermontov is fulfilling here precisely what Pushkin wrote Gnedich about already in 1821: "The scene of my narrative must be situated on the banks of the noisy Terek, on the borders of Georgia, in the deep gorges of the Caucasus; I have placed my hero on the monotonous plains where I myself spent two months."

35. It is characteristic that the plot situations in "The Boyar Orsha" are so indefinite that who Arseny really was at that moment when Orsha finds him with his daughter remains unclear, just as what happened to him after his flight from the monastery remains unclear. Apparently, he joins the band of "dashing comrades" right after this flight and comes to his beloved secretly as a fugitive. Meanwhile it is usually considered that Arseny is Orsha's servant. Relating the narrative poem Duchesne writes: "Arseny, a serf of the Boyar Orsha, was surprised by him with his daughter. The boyar commits him into the hands of a monastic court. Taken away in infancy from his family, which he never knew, the accused was raised by force in the monastery. Having purchased him here, Orsha took him home as a servant (the Russian translation, p. 89). In fact, Orsha bought him from a monk when he was a child and placed him in the monastery; there is not a word concerning "service" in the narrative poem.

36. I am employing Yu. Tynyanov's terminology, from his book *Problema stikhotvornogo iazyka* (Leningrad, "Academiia," 1924).

37. For example, "And death did not appear fearful" (The Novice) - "Death did not appear fearful to me" (The Beggar); "In the triumphant hour of praise" (The Novice) - "In the triumphant hour of prayer" (The Black Monk), etc.

38. There is a direct path from "The Novice" to Turgenev's narrative poem "A Conversation" (1844), where we have before us the already clear

decadence of the classical Russian verse line.

39. Evidently, the Demon.

40. See Duchesne's book and S. Shuvalov's article cited above.

41. It is interesting that in an 1833 sketch we find an even sharper passage in this respect, one which completely destroys the pathetic tone of the preceding lines:

> Простите, кроткие надежды
> Любви, блаженства и добра, -
> Открыл дремавшие он вежды...
> И то сказать - давно пора!

> Farewell, timid hopes
> Of love, happiness and goodness -
> He opened his slumbering eylids...
> *And it should be said - it's about time!*

42. This is the translation of the second part of Thomas Moore's *Lalla Rookh*, entitled "Paradise and the Peri" - Tr.

43. Compare in Podolinsky's "Borsky":

> Неизъяснимое волненье
> Объемлет душу; сожаленье
> Ему доступно - и лобовь
> Невольно в грудь теснится вновь.

> Inexpressible anxiety
> Envelopes his soul; regret
> Is open to him - and love
> Involuntarily crowds into his breast anew.

44. Recently this rhythmic-intonational device was revived and carried to its limits by A. Bely:

> В вас несвершаемые леты
> Неутоляемой алчбы -
> Неразрывные миголеты
> Неотражаемой судьбы...
> . . . .
> Невыразимая осанна,
> Неотразимая звезда
>
> . . . .

Я смыт вздыхающей волною
В неутихающий покой.

            ("Первое свидание," 1921 г.)

> In you there are uncompletable flights
> Of insatiable greed --
> Unbreakable momentary flights
> Of unreflectable fate....
>
> . . . .
> An inexpressible hosanna,
> An irresistible star
>
> . . . .
> I have been washed overboard by a pining wave
> Into an unsubsiding calm.
>
>   ("The First Rendezvous," 1921)

45. that is, "Vadim."

46. Besides Byron's "Childe Harold" (Canto IV, Stanzas 140-141), apparently the French poet Chênedollé's poem "Le gladiateur" was a source of this poem, as was pointed out by M. Breitman (*Vestnik literatury*, 1922, Nos. 2-3). Lermontov is closer to Chênedollé in details than to Byron. The name Chênedollé (Charles-Julien de Chênedollé, 1769 - 1833) was quite popular in Russia; Zhukovsky mentions him in his "Diary" among the authors whom he is translating.

47. In the history of Russian verse Lermontov doubtless must be regarded as a poet who strengthens and emphasizes the influence of euphony (here, seemingly, is one of the features linking him with the symbolists, and in particular with Bryusov. On this see V. Zhirmunsky's work "Valery Bryusov and the Legacy of Pushkin"). However, in the present work, at the center of which lies a literary historical problem, I intentionally am leaving this problem aside. A special investigation must be devoted to it and only then will the problem of euphony be moved from the dead center to which the eclectics and epigones of impressionistic criticism have brought it (and not the "formalists," as poorly-oriented reviewers and feuilletonists usually think). It is necessary to distinguish the functional meanings of different sound systems: declamatory-mimetic euphony, where expressive articulation comes to the fore, must be distinguished from sound-proper or "musical" euphony. For the scientific development of this division of poetics the elaboration of a corresponding theory is imperative; this theory is still lacking. (The works of Yakubinsky, Brik, Bernshtein, Artyushkov, and others only touch on general questions; they establish the very fact of the existence of a phonic organization in verse .)

48. Heine's "Sie liebten sich beide, doch keiner." - tr.

49. A detailed analysis of the composition of these poems by Zhukov-sky in connection with Lermontov's "A Branch of Palestine" was made in my book *Melodika stikha* (pp. 59-66). The very theme of a flower or a branch as material for this kind of meditations is very widespread in the poetry of this period. Pushkin's "The Flower" (1828) is very close to Musset's poem "A une fleur," although the latter was written later:

> Que me veux tu, chère fleurette,
> Aimable et charmant souvenir?
> Demi-morte et demi-coquette,
> Jusqu'à moi qui te fait venir?
>
> Sous ce cachet enveloppée,
> Tu viens de faire un long chemin.
> Qu'as tu vu? que t'a dit la main
> Qui sur le buisson t'a coupée
> > > > > etc.

50. Compare in "The Dying Gladiator": "the momentary amusement of an insensitive crowd," etc.

51. An indication of this connection was made by Yu. N. Tynyanov in his student paper ("The Literary Source of Lermontov's 'The Death of a Poet'"), which was read in S. A. Vengerov's seminar (1913).

52. Compare in the poem on the death of Pushkin:

> А вы, надменные потомки
> Известной подлостью прославленных отцов.
>
> A you, *haughty* offspring
> Of fathers *renowned for notorious baseness.*

53. Compare, for instance, Khomyakov's poem "The Dagger" (*Moskovskii Vestnik,* 1830, part III, No. 12) cited by N. Brodskii in the above-named article (page 106), and Lermontov's "The Dagger" (1837).

54. Critics reared on Pushkin's verse sharply felt the rhetorical quality of Lermontov's poetry and took note of his semantic eccentricities. In analyz-ing the poem "To the Memory of A. I. Odoevsky" Rozen stops, incidentally, on the line "Peace to your heart, my dear Sasha" and writes: "The diminu-tive has a special charm here. Extract this *one line* from the piece and it will

become something truly touching; like a gravestone inscription it will be sublimely simple and beautiful. But in the verses following thereafter this momentary feeling immediately is spent in an empty, inflated metaphor." In the concluding lines of "The 1st of January" ("O, how I would like to disrupt their merriment//And impertinently cast in their eyes an *iron* verse,//Dripping with bitterness and spite") Rozen indicates that "an iron verse, no matter what it is dripping with, is an unfortunate expression. Imagine spite in the form of a *liquid*: it will be *bile*! And now this bile, flowing along the iron stripe of the verse line, really is no good! But without this liquid the *iron* verse in itself is very good; and if it is still absolutely essential to add fuel and force to the fire, then heat it white-hot with spite or whatever you wish and dash it in the eyes of the sweet beauties greeting, like you, the New Year at the home of the hospitable N.N." About "A Prayer" ("I, Mother of God") Rozen writes: "In these florid lines there is neither sublime simplicity nor sincerity--the two main properties of a prayer! In praying for a *young* innocent maiden, is it not early to mention old age and even her death? Note: a *warm* defender of the *cold* world! What a cold antithesis!" (*Syn otechestva,* 1843, Book 3). It is interesting that Rozen appraises Marlinsky extraordinarily highly in this same article: "Pushkin made a fortunate expedition into the mountains with his 'The Prisoner of the Caucasus,' and the grandiose Marlinsky--the most brilliant of Russian writers--decisively conquered all this region and all the mountain-dwellers' nature, subdued *everything* to his genius, from the spirits of the highest mountains and the gnomes of the most hidden gorges to everything poetic and dashing in the mores and soul of the sons of the Caucasus! After *two* such geniuses what remained for a third poet blessed only with *talent*, although a very remarkable one?"

55. See B. Tomashevsky's book *Russkoe stikhoslozhenie* (Russian Institute of the History of the Arts, Petersburg, "Academiia," 1923), pp.62-64.

56. There is a detailed analysis of this in my book *Melodika stikha* (pp. 104-114).

57. The beginning of "A Fairytale for Children" (1839):

> Умчался век эпических поэм,
> И повести в стихах пришли в упадок.

> The age of epic poems has dashed away
> And tales in verse have fallen into decay.

58. Until now the title "Valerik," which was given by the publishers of the almanac *Utrenniaia zaria* (1843), has been maintained in all editions; this poem does not have a title in the author's manuscript, and to judge by its its character should not have one.

59. On the euphonic system of this poem see S. Durylin's article "The Academy Lérmontov and Lermontovian Poetics" (*Trudy i dni*, Notebook VIII, 1916) and A. Artiushkov's little book *Zvuk i stikh* (Petrograd: Seiatel', 1923), pp. 30-34.

60. There is a more detailed discussion on this in *Melodika stikha* (pp. 114-118). See also B. Tomashevskii. *Russkoe stikhoslozhenie* (pp. 47-48).

61. See I. N. Rozanov's interesting article "Echoes of Lermontov" (the collection *Venok M. Iu. Lermontovu*).

62. An analogous line is in Byron's "Beppo" (61):

> Crush'd was Napoleon by the northern Thor,
>> Who knock'd his army down with icy hammer,
>>> etc.

63. "Sashka," Stanza LXX:

> Он начал думать, строить мир воздушный,
> И в нем терялся мыслию послушной.
> Таков средь океана островок:
> Пусть хоть прекрасен, свеж, но одинок
>> и т. д.

> He began to think, to build an aerial world
> And lost himself in obedient thought in it.
> Such is an islet amidst the ocean
> Be it even beautiful, fresh, but solitary
>> etc.

"The First of January":

> И память их жива поныне
> Под бурей тягостных сомнений и страстей,
> Как свежий островок безвредно средь морей
> Цветет на влажной их пустыне.

> And their memory is alive today
> Under the storm of burdensome doubts and passions,
> As a fresh islet amidst the sea harmlessly
> Flowers on their moist desert.

64. These words, of course, are a parody on the solemn style, some-

thing in the nature of Pimen's words in *Boris Godunov*: "But day is near, the lamp burns down."

65. As L. Semenov has pointed out (*M. Iu. Lermontov. Stat'i i zametki* [M., 1915], pp. 251-52), this simile goes back to Milton's narrative poem "Paradise Lost." But it is characteristic that Lermontov distorts Milton's simile, not making that distinction between fruits grown near Sodom and which tempted only the eye, and the fruits of Hell which have deceived the taste, as was done in the original. Here is Milton's text ("Paradise Lost," Book X, v. 560-567):

> Greedily they pluck'd
> The fruitage, fair to sight, like that which grew
> Near that bituminous lake where Sodom flamed;
> This more delusive, not the touch, but taste
> Deceived: they fondly thinking to allay
> Their appetite with gust, instead of fruit
> Chew'd bitter ashes; which th' offended taste
> With spatt'ring noise rejected

66. "The Vampire. A Tale Related by Lord Byron." With the supplement of an excerpt from one of Byron's unfinished compositions. (From the English) *P. K.* Moscow, 1828. In the foreword it is stated that this tale was taken down from Byron's words by Doctor Polidori. I am grateful to T. A. Roboli for pointing this out.

67. Compare in "Sashka" (Stanza XCIX):

> Дремало все, лишь в окнах изредка
> Являлась свечка, силуэт рубчатый
> Старухи, из картин Рембрандта взятый,
>
> и т. д.

> Everything was dozing, only now and then in the windows
> A candle appeared, the ribbed silhouette
> Of an old woman, taken from Rembrandt's pictures,
> etc.

68. Compare in Gogol's "The Fair at Sorochinsk"(the end of chapter IX): "illuminated by spots of light burning uncertainly and timidly, they looked like a wild throng of gnomes surrounded by heavy subterranean steam

187

and clouds of gloom of a night from which there is no waking." Also in M. Zhukova's *Evenings on the Karpovka* (2nd edition, 1838, p. 42): "I loved these pictures. This flame, from time to time casting a bright light on the carts and drivers, who look like some kind of shadows suddenly appearing from the dark in their black shirts," etc. Here also is a traditional comparison with painting: "to me this all seemed like a picture worthy of the brush of Rembrandt, of Salvatore Roza, and my imagination was led out of the circle of ordinary life. Laugh, but I saw in the drivers both gnomes and subterranean dwellers of the legendary Tartarus." In western literature of the 40s this already was sensed as a banality. Compare in Bulwer's novel *The Disowned:* "Something there was in the scene...which (to use the orthodox phrase of the novelist) would not have been wholly unworthy the bold pencil of Salvatore himself" (chapter II).

69. See in detail my article "Pushkin's Path to Prose" *Pushkinskii sbornik pamiati Professora S. A. Vengerova,* Petersburg Gos. Izd-vo, 1923.

70. L. Maikov, *Pushkin*, pp. 418 and 423.

71. A manuscript article concerning Gogol's *Mirgorod* (P. Sakulin, *Iz istorii russkogo idealizma,* Vol. I, part 2, p. 385).

72. The article "On the Novel of N. Polevoi," 1833 (*Polnoe sobranie sochinenii,* 1838, part XI, p. 3I6).

73. "The First Letter of Three Tver' Landowners to Baron Brambeus" (*Biblioteka dlia chteniia,* 1837, Vol. XXII, and *Sobranie sochinenii,* Vol.VIII, pp. 200-235).

74. Ibid.

75. *Polnoe sobranie sochinenii,* Vol. II, p. 375.

76. The article on Bulgarin's "Mazeppa" in *Biblioteka dlia chteniia 1834, II (Sobranie sochinenii,* 1859, Vol. VIII,pp. 44 and 46).

77. P. Sakulin, *Iz istorii russkogo idealizma,* Vol. I, part 2, p. 388.

78. The article "What is a Novel" in *Otechestvennye zapiski,* 1839, Vol. V, p. 79.

79. The article is published in *Sovremennik* (1836, Book III) under the title "How We Write Novels." I am quoting the manuscript text from P. Sakulin's book.

80. *Gimnaziia vysshikh nauk i litsei kn. Bezborodko,* 2nd edition, St. Petersburg, 1881, p. 306.

81. See V. Shklovskii's book *"Tristram Shendi" Sterna i teoriia romana.*

82. This description of Sennaya Square was so popular that the anonymous author of the verse novel *Polina* (1839), describing this same Sennaya, interrupted the description with a reference to Marlinsky:

Посуда на сенной пестреет,
Пестреют люди на Сенной,
Ряды свининой богатеют,
Телеги тянутся толпой;
Чистосердечные телята
Лежат, не чуя мясников,
На задних лапках поросята
Висят среди окороков;
Говядина, дичь и копченья,
Грибы, капуста, все здесь есть;
Но чтоб избегнуть повторенья,
Прошу Марлинского прочесть.

Plates and dishes appear motley on the Sennaya,
People are motley on the Sennaya,
Rows of stalls are rich with pork,
Carts string out in a crowd;
Simple-hearted calves
Lie not sensing the butchers,
Suckling pigs by their hind feet
Hang amidst hams;
Beef, wildfowl, and smoked foods,
Mushrooms, cabbages, everything is here;
But in order to avoid repetition,
I beg you to read Marlinsky.

83. On the margins of the copy belonging to the Pushkin House characteristic remarks were made by some reader: to the words "Where is Iva?"-- "It's high time!" and further on--"this one is Bayan, but not Vel'tman!" (I, 139).

84. See A. Tseitlin's work *Povesti o bednom chinovnike Dostoevskogo*, M., 1923.

85. Compare in *Vadim* "an entire future shone in his eyes."

86. Compare in *Vadim*: "He was sitting and sobbing, paying no attention either to the sister or the deceased. God alone knows what was then occurring in the hunchback's soul, because, having covered his face with his hands, he did not utter a single word further." (Chapter XX).

87. And further: "in simple hearts the feeling of the beauty and grandeur of nature is stronger, a hundred-fold more lively, than in us, enraptured storytellers in words and on paper."

88. Compare, for example, the author's acquaintance with his hero in Brentano's novel *Godwi*, where play with illusion and motivation occurs all

189

the time. (L. Lunt's report, read at "OPOYAZ".)

89. There was no introductory preface in the first edition of *A Hero of Our Time* (1840); it appeared in the second edition (1841) in response to criticism and landed, probably for technical reasons, at the beginning of the second part, i.e., before "Princess Mary" (with special pagination).